We Said Yes!

Stephen James Hogue

with
Bruce Wetter

Table of Contents

Preface

When I met Stephen, I was in my junior year of college. We established a relationship based on a strong friendship, which then led to courtship and marriage, all within a 14-month time frame. By the time I graduated with my bachelor's degree in psychology, I was engaged. Three months later, we tied the knot, and the day after our return from honeymoon, I began the arduous journey of a master's program in social work.

Meanwhile, Stephen was a full-time youth pastor. We lived in a tiny apartment while he worked hard at paying my way through grad school. With some scholarships and grant money added to that, I completed my graduate studies without debt. Meanwhile, we scraped pennies to make ends meet to pay rent and buy groceries. After grad school, I worked full-time, and we put aside my entire salary in a savings account. We figured that since we could live on Steve's income alone, we would continue that meager lifestyle in order to save up for a house. Our idea was that we would start a family once we settled into our own home.

As a little girl, I grew up dreaming of marriage and a family early on. As the oldest of four, I took on the 'mommy' role with my sisters. I had no doubt that one day I would marry young and start a family right away. I wanted it more than anything else in the world! I thought about the little faces that would have daddy's nose and my curly hair; patience like my husband's and gratitude for the little things in life like I learned when I met Jesus. I imagined that one of our children would have light eyes like my mother-in-law and tan skin like my Egyptian side of the family. I desired to have three biological children and adopting one internationally. Plans on four children seemed large at the time. But Stephen agreed, and we had talked about our future children even during our courting months.

After five years of renting our little apartment, we moved from Orlando to Ormond Beach, FL. Stephen took a position as a full-time children's pastor while I obtained a position as a guidance counselor in the school system. With the money we saved up while living in our tiny apartment, we put a downpayment on our first home.

I felt like it was a good time for us to begin a family. We had health insurance for the first time and now owned a three-bedroom, two-bath house with lots of room to grow!

One year passed of trying to conceive, and using all of the off the counter devices and contraptions to decipher ovulation cycles, we gave up and sought help. We were referred to a fertility specialist, who did the bloodwork and the proper testing to figure out the issue. Besides a slightly low sperm count, nothing else could be pinpointed. We were given the diagnosis "unknown infertility."

It was a frustrating diagnosis, to say the least. What do you do to "fix "unknown infertility? We would have much rather a diagnosis that could have a cure or treatment than one that didn't make any sense.

After taking medication, undergoing five rounds of artificial insemination, and having surgery to investigate what could be going on with my inward female anatomy, we weren't any closer to an answer. With no results, we decided to get a second opinion.

We learned about a fertility specialist in Jacksonville, Florida, an hour and a half away from where we lived. After consultation, we felt like this doctor was an answer to prayer. He did some other tests and sonograms and diagnosed me with cervical stenosis, which is a closed womb, as the Bible refers to it. No other issues. No other diagnosis. The doctor linked it to a congenital disability. Something I was born with that was not associated with any pain or symptoms. Just the fact that one day, unbeknownst to me, I would struggle with having babies.

My new fertility specialist, Dr. Brown, was convinced that a simple surgery to put a stent in the cervix would allow the sperm in and have a chance at conception. However, under sedation, Dr. Brown decided to physically open the cervix and not put the stent in. It was staying open on its own, which seemed to resolve the issue. We were encouraged to try to conceive within six months of the surgery.

Six months came and went.

Then one year.

Then two.

Stephen and I decided to no longer funnel funds into conceiving and discontinue any further treatments, medicine, or surgeries. We would leave it up to God to do a miracle if He so chose.

This was a closed door for us in the natural. In the meantime, God was working something differently in our lives. By the time we were in our tenth year of marriage, we had already fostered 10 children and adopted four – one from a private agency. We fostered more kids and two years later, we adopted two more. In our 16th year of being married, we adopted a newborn from a private agency and a toddler from foster care. Three years after that, we finalized the adoption of a sibling group and added them to our family. Our home had a revolving door with some foster children staying a week, or close to two years, or forever.

And just like that, we became a family of 12! This was not in OUR plans at all! These were not OUR dreams. Along the way, we realized that our journey wasn't about conception. It wasn't about fostering in order to adopt. It was about dreaming with God that orphans would find a family. That fatherless children would have a mother and a father who would point them to their heavenly Father. It was about a search and rescue mission. It was about a calling from God. Redemption. Restoration. Obedience.

It wasn't about Stephen and Sandra at all. Our only role was that we lay down our own dreams to fulfill God's. It's the most difficult, yet most fulfilling part of our lives!

So, here we are... married now for 22 years. Twelve

children, ages 6 to 20. The children God put in our home, are no longer orphans. They are HIS children. They are Hogue children.

Wanted. Chosen. Loved. Valuable. Precious.

Join us on this journey of marriage, ministry, infertility, foster care, and adoption. And ask yourself the question, "What is God calling me to do?". And then do it.

Sandra Hogue

Chapter One

Silas

July, 2004

My wife is a beautiful woman. Her beauty starts deep within and bubbles outward, and I consider myself most blessed of men that God has seen fit to make us one. We live in the wonderful community of Ormond Beach, Florida, and have perhaps the perfect job—we are children's pastors for a large and thriving church.

Or perhaps I should say, it was the perfect job three years ago when we were hired. Not that the job changed. It didn't. Nor did Calvary Christian Center, a wonderful place filled with people doing their best to shine Christ's light into the community. No, it was us, Sandra and I. It wasn't something we did, but something we couldn't do—have children.

We had waited on the decision to start a family, wanting first to find the stability a family would require—a job we loved, a church we fit with, a marriage that had proven God's blessing. And then we waited some more. Months passed, then a year. We went to an infertility doctor. He recommended surgery, but after four hours under sedation, he couldn't find what he was looking for. So we went to another. We undertook various treatments. Finally, after only a year, Sandra and I accepted the advice that she should go in for a second surgery. Two painful and nerve-racking surgeries later. Both were very costly procedures with five days of recovery each time, neither fully covered by insurance. So, now we're out of money and have no baby.

Back to square one.

Now we find, a blessed job has become a test. Our work as children's pastors a pesky reminder of our failure, a constant fight against the demons of disappointment and frustration. To make matters worse, like rubbing salt into an open wound, everyone around us is getting pregnant. I am a man of God, I believe in divine healing. I believe with all my heart and soul that God is great, that He can work wonders. So why hasn't He? Is our faith somehow lacking? Is this a punishment? Have we been found not worthy of bringing children into this world? I have worn out my knees in prayer, searching for answers, but all I'm left with are questions.

The single paycheck we receive for our work at Calvary is unquestionably adequate but doesn't allow us to consider the expense of private adoption. Instead, we sign up to be foster parents, hoping perhaps to adopt in that way. We go through a forest of paperwork, attend 30 hours of training sessions, open our home to inspection by strangers, and do everything else required. The process seems endless. Maybe the fault is mine, for deep in my heart, I still believe my wife will conceive. I still believe that she'll be wheeled out of the hospital holding the flesh of our flesh, that friends and relatives will argue over whose nose the little one has, whose mouth, whose ears.

Little did I realize as we dress for church this last Sunday in July of 2004 what a miracle God has in store for us.

* * *

Calvary Christian Center is a busy place, especially on a Sunday. As on most Sundays, Sandra and I have our hands full running the children's ministry department, a job that, despite our personal difficulties, is both glorious and fulfilling. *Let the little children come to me*, Jesus said. In the presence of children, it takes a heart of stone not to feel God's glory all around. Still, it can be daunting, as when I hear little Shelby Watson say to my wife, "Miss Sandra, Miss Sandra, come and see my new baby brother!"

My wife lets Shelby pull her out to a waiting car, where Jack—a judge in our area—and his wife Sharon greet her, bubbling on like new parents tend to do about the week-old boy they've just adopted. I wander over and glance in. A beautiful boy, I can't help thinking. I hear Sandra say, "We'd like to adopt... but it's so expensive. Stephen and I have decided to become foster parents. Maybe we'll adopt the kids we foster."

"You want to adopt?" Jack says. "Got all your papers filled out?"

Sandra leans into the car, cooing at the baby, hardly listening. "We just got done with the home inspection," she says absently. "That was the last requirement. We're waiting for our foster care license to be approved and sent from Tallahassee."

Jack smiles. He's beaming, really. "Good," he says. "Because there's another little boy down at the hospital. They're looking to place him immediately. Another family is in line before you, but... are you interested if they change their minds?"

"Yes!" Even from behind her, I can feel the warmth of her smile. "For sure!

"Okay, I'll give them a call. As I said, there's another family considering the boy—but if they say no, be ready. The attorney wants a placement as quickly as possible. Poor kid. His mom left as soon as he was born, didn't even give him a name. She signed away her parental rights, so there won't be any legal fuss."

We go home and rest, which is what we do after two long services with setting up and clean up, totaling a six-hour day. On this particular day, Sandra is also getting ready to start a new job as a guidance counselor at a nearby elementary school. And I am packing to leave on a trip to Kids Camp. Both of us are too busy to entertain conversations with each other about the possibility of the baby. Not to mention, we're quite sure that the other couple will adopt the baby.

The next morning is hectic. I'm leaving for the church's annual Kids Camp—thirty kids with me for five days at a camp about three hours away. Florida, despite its growing population, is still mostly a thicket of forested wilderness. Okay, it's a wilderness that's never terribly far away from a 7/11, but in the eyes of a child, it's a new world, a mysterious world, clear proof that God is the greatest of creators. And Kids Camp promises to be a lot of work for me. Thirty kids

4

never want to all do the same thing or walk in the same direction. It's like letting the ants out of an ant farm. I have my hands full. There's little time to think about yesterday's conversation with Judge Watson. Or any need to—the other family has obviously said yes to the little boy.

The camp, located on thirty acres, has a wandering cell phone reception area about the size of a closet. While out swimming or supervising games, I do my best to find that hidden closet, to call home, but to no avail. Sandra has, on the surface at least, written off the possible adoption. "Unplanned," I hear her say, holding up one finger. "Not included in our budget"; another finger. "And I just started a new job." Strike three. She does her best to smile. She's always been the practical one. Still, under her pretense, I know she's hurting.

On the second day of camp, while out in one of the fields, I am surprised to see the camp director's wife hurrying towards me. I'm thinking she's tired of desk work and wants a change of scenery, but upon arriving, she pants out that there's an emergency message to call my wife.

I sprint back to the payphone in the hallway outside the gymnasium, praying Sandra's not hurt, praying for all those I've left behind, praying that everything is fine with her new job. But when I hear her, she's anything but sad. "They changed their minds!" Her voice has the timbre of a jet pulling away from the ground, soaring upwards. "The other family! The attorney wants to know if we're still interested."

For a moment, all I can do is hold onto the phone,

afraid that if I let go, all this will disappear. "They... what?"

Sandra ignores my piercingly perceptive question, tells me that we both need to get to the hospital in Orlando. ASAP.

The camp director is kind enough to find another counselor willing to take on my kids, allowing me to leave. I try not to speed. I try not to notice the hammering of my heart. I meet Sandra at the hospital entrance. Together, we hurry to the Neonatal Intensive Care Unit. In the minutes it takes us to get there, I doubt either of us draws in a complete breath.

However, as much of a rush we're in, the adoption attorney will not let us see the baby until we've talked with her. She's of medium build, weary blue eyes, hair-sprayed blonde hair, she introduces herself, then shocks us by saying that the baby weighs only three pounds, eleven ounces. "Full-term," she says. "Just a low birth weight. No one knows why. We have almost no medical information on the parents, the mother signed away her rights shortly after the baby's birth, then disappeared."

Her brow furrows into a series of craggy lines, eyes coming alive, lasering in on us. "I'll give you fifteen minutes with the baby. After that, it's either yes or no. This baby needs a family. If you don't want him, we'll try someone else."

Fifteen minutes seems like an absurd amount of time for a decision that will last a lifetime, but we're in no position to argue. Sandra and I nod, then nervously wash before entering the NICU.

The room is a large rectangle with small incubator-beds and a whole lot of specialty baby-saving equipment lining the walls of the room. There are perhaps a dozen babies in the room. All have family members standing around them, gaily colored balloons festooning the air, stuffed animals seated on tables, prominent tags displaying child's and parent's names taped onto the incubators.

Then we see him, the cubicle furthest away, and our hearts break. He's alone, crying, no visitors, no balloons, no stuffed bears—and no name on his name tag. Wires and monitors held on by surgical tape cover his tiny body. We move closer, see a single splash of color, a tiny blue and pink-lined white beanie cap covering his head. And that's all it takes to make him absolutely adorable.

"Can I pick him up?" my wife asks, already leaning over.

"No, of course not," the nurse on duty tells us, her words clipped. "Only family members can touch the children."

"But he has no family members," my wife says. The nurse remains silent. "Do you mean no one touches him?" Sandra's voice is soft with incredulity. Then, stronger, "I need to hold him, please. We are prospective parents. If we're going to adopt him, that's what I need please."

The nurse shrugs. "Let me talk to my supervisor." She turns, walking quickly away.

I looked at the tiny baby, then glance at the blank sheet of paper, then at the baby again. And I pray a simple prayer. Let us name him, Lord. Let us name him and nurture him and help him grow.

Without my noticing, the nurse has returned. "My super says you can hold him," she tells us as she leans down, carefully lifting the baby. It's a difficult task, for a myriad of wires attached to machines have to be brought along. As he's lifted, the child's crying rises to a wailing scream. So little and so fragile, but plenty of noise. Sandra takes him, cuddling him against her chest. "Are you my baby?" she coos. "Did God choose you for us?" And just like that, the crying stops, a look of peace coming into the baby's face.

Prayer answered.

I hear a tapping on the cubicle's observation window, and looking up, see my mother staring in through the glass. My parents live in Orlando. They must have arrived shortly after us. Her lips are moving, but I can't hear the words. Realizing my problem, she slowly mouths the words. "That's... my... grandbaby!"

"What do you think?" Sandra says to me.

I turn back to her, watch the tiny creation in her arms coo and burble, the smallest baby I've ever seen. We have no medical history, no idea why the birth weight is so low, what problems this child will encounter as a result. Despite these thoughts, a feeling of contentment settles over me, a calmness and love that I see reflected in my wife's face. "Why would we say no?" I tell her. "This is exactly what we've been praying for. God has given us a family."

We return to the attorney, give her an enthusiastic yes, at which point we are joined by the hospital's social worker, who has us sign our names on various documents. Once finished, the social worker asks us if we have a name for the baby. My wife and I exchange broad smiles. "Silas," we say at the same moment. It's a name God had given us seven years before when we thought our first children would be twins, Silas and Selah. For a moment, I wonder where Selah is and when we'll meet her.

For now, though, just Silas. "Silas James Hogue," I say. The social worker smiles as she pulls out a Polaroid camera, snapping a photo of us. As it turns from gloss black to colors, she writes the name Silas on a piece of paper, and our names next to it. Then into the NICU, down to the very last cubicle, taping the photo and names to it. Balloons and stuffed animals will soon follow. I'm sure my Father is rejoicing, for this lost baby has now been found.

The hospital has rules, and one of them is that babies must weigh four pounds before the parents can take them home. So Sandra and I, as well as several family members, take turns staying with our new baby boy. Down the street from the hospital, we stay at the Ronald McDonald House for a few nights. It's a two-story motel-like building, where parents can stay for a small fee while their child is in the hospital. We walk over several times a day, talk to him, hold him, pray over him, sing to him. His first eight days might have been a little slow, but now the love and laughter are pouring in. He begins to gain weight, and five days after we said *yes*, he hits the four-pound mark. By this time, his cubicle is filled with presents from friends and family. I doubt there has ever been a more beautiful, glowing mom than Sandra, as she picked up our tiny bundle for the trip home.

"I'm afraid you can't just walk out," a nurse says. I

can feel my heart thud, but then I see her bring out a wheelchair. Another hospital rule—all new moms need to be wheeled out. I'm not sure if she's serious, but Sandra's game. She sits, holding Silas, leaving me to hurry behind, my arms full of baby stuff.

A nurse walking the hall in the opposite direction does a double-take, for Sandra sports perfectly applied makeup, weighs all of one-hundred pounds, and looking absolutely stunning. "You did *not* just have that baby!" she says. And we all begin laughing.

At the door of the hospital, it hits me—this is our baby. God has given us this precious baby to love and nurture and protect. I'm suddenly aware that I need to open every door carefully, looking both ways, perform my fatherly tasks without flaw or fault. No mistakes. None. I'll be a good Dad; Sandra will be a great Mom. With God's help.

Boy, do I have a lot to learn.

Chapter Two

Sandra and Stephen

For both Sandra and I, life has been an overflow of blessings and struggle. We rarely think of the years going by because we rarely have the time. Most days are a deluge of challenging situations, demands, heartbreak, and triumph in equal measure. Ten children will do that to you. Despite this, time does pass, evidenced by what seems like weekly trips to shoe stores for larger sizes. Through it all, Sandra's spirit continues to shine, her smile still eager, her eyes still lustrous, and her laugh...well, her laugh is a glory and a gift from God. It's also how we met. Or, at least, how I met her. I'm still not sure if she ever noticed me.

I was nineteen, attending a retreat for young adults being held at one of the local beaches. During a mid-morning service, my attention was distracted by someone laughing—which was odd, because everyone was laughing, the speaker was a funny guy. But this particular laughter soared, spun around itself, playful and delighting, and despite trying to concentrate on the sermon, I found myself waiting for it, lingering in it when it came, like some wonderful new smell that vitalized the very air that held it.

A short while later, I met the girl behind the laugh. If I had been distracted before, I was now mesmerized, captivated by her beauty—not a done up, painted on beauty, but a Spirit-dwelling, love of the Lord beauty radiating from every word she spoke, every move she made. Her parents had emigrated from Egypt in the early '70s, then divorced when she was six. Raised by her hardworking mom, she grew up in South Florida with two younger sisters.

And then the conference ended. I went my way, she went hers. That's how life goes when you're nineteen.

Fortunately for us, God is a bit more farsighted. He's also the perfect matchmaker—doesn't charge much, works day and night, and never has to offer a money-back guarantee, because He never makes a mistake. Sandra moved to Orlando to attend college, and needing a church, she opened the phone book and picked one at random. In a city with more churches than I can name, she chose the very one I attended.

Still, it was a congregation of five thousand, many people attended for years without knowing that their neighbors down the street also attended. But Sandra didn't want to simply go to church, she wanted to serve her church. Which was exactly how I felt. She decided to become a youth leader. The same decision I'd made. She got involved in the youth ministry. As I had. And before too many weeks had passed, she and I and a great group of friends were hanging out pretty much all the time - at church functions, birthday parties, fellowship groups. What I liked best was the lack of pressure—we were all friends, free to have fun, grow in the Lord and get to know one another as the special people God had created us to be.

Which is when I decided to blow it. That's me, Stephen Hogue - sometimes I have all the patience of a rock rolling downhill.

* * *

The core of my relationship with Sandra was friendship. We felt comfortable sharing stories of past relationships, why they had gone wrong, what we had learned, and what we were searching for in a life mate. Sandra told of her pledge to the Lord—she was no longer going to date just to be dating. The next man she dated regularly would become her husband. I admired this about her, this surety of purpose. Why not? As I said, we were friends, nothing more.

My approach to dating was somewhat more haphazard, what I would like to call spontaneous, free-form, go with the flow. In other words, I rarely thought about consequences, or taking my time to develop a rapport, or seeking advice. Going slow was something I could do later... say, in about forty or fifty years.

At the time, I lived with a friend in an apartment complex. Sandra started to come over with meals, and while she was there, she would do some cleaning, some mending, the day-to-day details that I never much thought about. If my friend or I got sick, Sandra would bring us chicken noodle soup; if either of us needed a ride, she was there; if there was some problem I wanted to discuss, her time was my time. She had that kind of heart. So, naturally, I asked her out on a date.

I mean, why else would anyone be so generous? In my self-absorption, I thought, wow, she must really, really like me - pretty clear that she thought of me as future husband material.

Turned out, she did like me - but as she explained, her voice kind and patient, she liked everyone. She gave freely to everyone. Without dating them, she added pointedly.

It was a blow to my pride, to be sure. But more than that, it pointed out my spiritual immaturity, for what I had failed to see in Sandra was blatantly obvious - her very nature, God-given and glowing, was compassionate, generous, loving. To misinterpret these traits as singularly meant for me ... well, I had a lot to learn, didn't I?

And I intended to learn it. I worked hard to regain Sandra's trust and friendship to become the type of person she could respect. She was disciplined, consistent, hard-working. Compared to Sandra's life, mine was a disorganized mess! She was also confident, a trait to which I could hardly lay claim. Over time, I learned to be there for her as she was there for me. I learned what she already knew - how to be a friend. And that is what we became, the best of friends.

One evening, my parents invited me over for dinner. My sister and her husband would also be there. I asked Sandra if she wanted to go. There was nothing more to it than that. It would be a good meal, pleasant conversation, a nice time. Just one friend sharing his family with another friend.

Of course, that was before my father met us at the door. He took one look at Sandra, gave her a big hug, a happy grin, and a boisterous welcome as if he'd known her all her life. Known her and cherished her. It was a little weird, but, hey, fathers can be that way.

Apparently, so can mothers, for upon being introduced to Sandra, my mom gave her the same big hug, a smile wide as the sky, and a "Hi, Sweetie, I'm glad you came!"

Hi, Sweetie? Sandra looked at me, smiling - I mean, who wouldn't be smiling? But also a little freaked out. And then my sister and her husband came along. You guessed it, the same hugs, smiles, all one big happy family. Which would have been fine, but then my brother-in-law leans towards Sandra, and in a whisper loud enough for all to hear, says, "You'll love the Hogues, they're *great* in-laws." I was appalled, somewhere north of letting my mouth drop open, but still south of swallowing my tongue. That would have to wait until after the meal.

Sure enough, after the meal, while I was helping my mom clean up, I noticed Sandra had disappeared. So had my father. This couldn't be good. I set off in search of them, heard laughter coming from the family room, where I discovered my dad showing Sandra an old VHS tape of me shaving for the first time, wearing nothing but my... well, let's just say it was definitely half-past swallow-my-tongue time.

On the way home, I apologized profusely to Sandra, I told her that my parents had never done anything like that before, that I hadn't said anything about her other than she was a friend I worked with in the youth ministry. She was gracious in her response, telling me that, really, it was fine.

Later - much later, after Sandra and I had been married - I asked my dad about that strange night, why he'd acted in such a peculiar way. "Stephen," he said, "when Sandra walked through our door, I knew her." When I pointed out that he couldn't possibly have known her, she hadn't grown up anywhere near Orlando, he simply told me, "I knew her... because that's the girl, I'd been praying you'd meet ever since you were born."

Wow.

Sandra and I on our wedding day.

Chapter Three

Stephen and Seth

July, 2005

I'm totally excited, more excited than I've ever thought possible. In two short days, Silas will turn one year old. A birthday! My son will be having a birthday! I buy balloons, toys, I pester Sandra about the cake. Vanilla or chocolate? Or are those too plain? Maybe a rainbow cake, or a jungle with a waterfall of icing.

"It's a smash cake!" Sandra tells me. "Most of it will end up on the floor!"

Just then, the phone rings. We're expecting a small army of birthday celebrants, all wanting to bring presents, supplies. "Stephen Hogue here," I announced cheerily. "Birthday Central."

"Congratulations!" The voice on the other end is familiar, but not very. It takes me a moment to realize it's Beth, our foster parent licensing agent. "Are you ready for this, Stephen? Is Sandra there?" Without waiting for an answer, she says, 'You are now officially licensed foster parents! Isn't that wonderful?"

"Yes, it's..."

"And we have two boys for you. Can we bring them over this afternoon?"

This afternoon? Now, somewhere in my birthday-addled brain, I know this isn't how it's supposed to be. The process, as it was described to us in our foster parent training, is one where we sit down with the case manager, talk about who the children are, their needs, their problems, their backgrounds, if they're a good match to fit into our family. Not "*we'll bring them over this afternoon*". But our prayer has been, "Father, bring us children." Well, here they come.

"The state investigator will bring them over at about three. You're exactly what these kids need!" she gushes.

At three, we're peeking out the second-story window, Sandra holding Silas, awaiting our new arrivals. One big happy family. The case worker's car pulls up, and we meet him at the front door. Justin, age 5 has no expression, as if he doesn't know what's going on. The other boy, Daen, a year younger, has to be dragged in, kicking and screaming. Both boys are dressed in mismatched clothing and wear dirty, worn shoes. Their heads have been shaved, their arms and legs are covered with bruises. The investigator brings in a cigarette-smoke smelled duffle bag with a few items he'd picked up from their house.

Sandra tries to ease Daen with a soft voice and he softens up and quiets down when he sees how peaceful Silas is. It's as if he thinks that if the baby is okay, this must a safe home and he will be okay too. We're told the boys will be with us for six months, maybe less if the father gets himself straightened out quicker. Then the investigator leaves, with a cheery "Don't worry, this is the perfect home for them. Perfect!" We find out much later that the boys were promised Disney World. Instead, they got us. No wonder Daen was screaming. Anger. Disappointment.

And then we're alone. "Anybody hungry?" Sandra says. Justin looks at Daen, then at us. "Brother wants a snack." We show them our refrigerator. They simply stare into it. They've never eaten a vegetable. Never. They can't even name most of the items on the shelves. They definitely knew what ketchup was. And Cheerios. If their father didn't bring home fast food and soft drinks, they went searching for the ketchup packets and the dry cereal.

Next, we take them to the room we've prepared. They stare at the floor, for that's where they're accustomed to sleeping. I smile as I show them their bunk beds, and ask them who wants to sleep where. But inwardly, my heart is breaking. At the same time, I'm praising God. The investigator might have meant it only as a well-practiced getaway line, but he was right—this *is* the perfect home for them.

The next week is busy. More than busy. Daen says almost nothing, while Justin talks nonstop, often telling us what 'brother' wants. "Brother is thirsty, brother wants the bathroom, brother wants to know if...." Both boys have problems with their teeth—Daen's are so decayed that some have to be pulled immediately. Which hardly helps us build a relationship. Promised Disney World, given the dentist. They also both have vision problems and need glasses. It's obvious, as they both squint their eyes to look 5 feet ahead of them.

There are also a few other problems. Hygiene and manners are words without meaning to Justin and Daen—they grab food with dirty hands, they have no concept of forks and spoons, or for that matter, of plates or napkins. If not watched closely, they will hoard food—we find forgotten remnants under pillows, in the closet, stuffed into pockets. They are unruly, badly educated, and consistently disobedient. Oh, and they lie with the ease and practice of hardened criminals.

The problem underlying all the other problems is that the boys have been told they'll someday go back with their father. This creates an almost unbearable tension for them. All children want and need loving and caring parents. At the same time, Justin and Daen know what they had with their father, and they know what they have with us. And they know that, despite anything Sandra or I say, they can be dragged out of here as quickly as they were dragged in. Just another lie of Disney World. At the end of the day, Sandra and I are no more than caretakers to them, no more than well-meaning strangers who haven't the power to keep them safe, or for that matter, to keep them at all.

This is the mindset we've challenged ourselves to change. God has given us the love and ability—but the process is so much harder than with a newborn baby. Despite his low birth weight and probable future medical problems, Sandra and I bonded instantly with Silas. But how do parents bond with kids who, in large part, are correct in what they think—they *can* be dragged out at any moment. Sandra and I do everything possible to soothe their fears... but what can we do about *our* fears? God gives, and God takes away. The giving part is hard enough, the staggering responsibility is loving and remolding these two little human beings. What will we do if someone takes them away?

Or should I say, *when* they take them away. The foster agency has told us that the boys will be with us no longer than six months. The plan is to return them to their father once he cleans up his act. The answer is not an easy one. We pray, we have faith that we said yes for a reason. What that reason it might be beyond our understanding. But it is not beyond His.

For the first two months, the father does well, showing up promptly for his weekly supervised visits with the kids, as well as complying with the other requirements the agency has given him. Then the excuses start. He tells the case worker that the time is inconvenient, he's out looking for a job, his car's broken down. Then he simply doesn't show up at all. Nothing the case worker hasn't seen dozens of times before.

Nothing Justin and Daen haven't seen before either. More disappointment. More adults lying to them. "This is your home," we tell them. "If it's our home," Justin asks, "how come brother and I can't live here forever?" "Because your father is getting better," Sandra and I tell them. "He loves you and wants you to live with him." That's an answer the boys have heard so often that their eyes actually roll to the side. Ketchup packets and stale cereal without milk. Better. Sure, if you say so.

The boys are confused, I understand that. And why not? *I'm* confused. We've been told six months. The *date* comes and goes, but the *boys* are staying.

Meanwhile, after a diligent search, their biological mother is located in Texas. She has no idea that after she left the house in the middle of the night, taking their sister with her, the boys were taken into the State's custody. She and her new husband decide they will work to get the boys transferred to Texas. Monthly phone "visits" begin with the woman the boys call Mom but don't remember. She left when they were two and three years old.

A year of foster care passes. Then a year and a half. During this time, we enroll Justin and Daen in school, we take them to the dentist, to the doctor, to therapy sessions. We buy them clothes, we teach them proper hygiene, manners, rules. And one other lesson, the hardest of all for them—we teach them love.

Or just possibly, His plan is for them to teach *us* love. For me, it's a struggle. Sandra and I want to believe we're making a difference, that we're doing God's work. But there's very little sign of it. Justin and Daen simply will not obey. This is especially true with Justin. I tell him to clean his room. It remains messy. I tell him to wash his hands before dinner. It's obvious he didn't use soap. I tell him to close the refrigerator door when he's finished, but there it is, open every time I visit the kitchen. I tell, and I tell, and I tell, and I tell, all of it wasted breath. He's defiant and disobedient, and his brother follows his lead.

After several months, I begin to see the writing on the wall—the only one changing is me, and not for the better. I catch myself yelling at the boys, I catch myself making mental lists of their wrongs, all the ways they are falling below expectations. When I tally it up, there's really not much I like about them.

Then I find out that Justin is failing in school. He's going to be held back. I take it personally. What will people think? But I know what they'll think—they'll think I'm a lousy foster Dad. It's probably all for the better that I didn't have natural children. Look at what a mess I'm making of it. Probably better that I simply call up the case worker, tell her she's made a mistake, we can't do it, find the boys another home.

In fact, we do just that. Sandra feels the same. Maybe the boys just aren't a good fit for our family. Sandra calls and asks that the boys be removed. Her voice steady as she says the words, but she can feel the shame roiling in her stomach. Sandra gets off the phone with a disappointed look on her face. The case worker tells her that we're doing quite well, better than anyone in the office thought we would. She says the case worker asks us to stick it out a little longer. That we are being tested.

Tested. She doesn't mean it the way I take it, but that hardly matters. It's as if I hear my Heavenly Father say, "Are you willing to become like me? How many times have I showered you with love that you didn't deserve? How many times have you turned away from me when I have never once turned away from you? Do you think I wasn't hurt? Do you think I actually *liked* your bad behavior? Even then, I showed you only love. Even now."

This is my test, then. To show love even when I don't feel it. To know that the love is real. Not my love, better than my love, a Light given from above. Week by week, month after month, the love I show these boys—

playing ball with them, taking them to buy new shoes, even telling them that, "no", they can't talk that way or act that way—slowly, the love takes root, grows inward, filling my heart. Week by week, month after month—I pray the boys would accept this gift, hold it close. I know *I* do. For I begin to see them not as the little lawbreakers they are, but as the wondrous creations my Father has envisioned. The same as He sees me. And from time to time, I actually catch myself thinking, *How lucky am I?*

* * *

Having a twelve-month-old baby in the house with a couple of misbehaving ruffians is, at first, a cause for vigilance and concern. Whenever the boys are around Silas, we monitor them closely. But instead of causing any kind of jealousy or problem, the presence of a 'baby brother' seems to be a point of reassurance for the boys. Maybe it's because they can see that Silas is well cared for and safe. Perhaps they like being able to care for a being even more in need than they. Maybe playing with a baby, cooing and crawling alongside him, letting him crawl on them, is their chance to be babies themselves. A process they didn't get much of an opportunity to enjoy.

The longer Justin and Daen stay, the more we are treated to a vision of what type of children they could become. Nightly, Sandra and I pray that a way is found for the boys to stay forever. Apparently, God agrees with us, for after two years, we get the news—the father's parental rights have been terminated, and the mother has voluntarily relinquished hers. Which means they need new parents. Which means...

"Boys," Sandra says after we sit them down, take our seats opposite them. "Boys." She can't hide the smile on her face. In a tender voice, she says, "If the judge says it's okay, would you like this to be your real home? I mean, your permanent home?" And when they don't quite get it, "Not a foster home anymore, but... your forever home?'

"Yes!" they scream together. "Yes! Yes! Yes!"

We've taught them about screaming in the house, how it isn't a good idea. But this time I'm the worst of examples, hollering along with them, reaching over, hugging them close. It's a time of joy. Absolute joy. I remember the day they arrived, the astounding changes they've gone through. As Christ promised, they are new beings, shiny with life. They are lost sheep come home. They are my sons.

Then I start thinking—when Sandra and I are granted the right to adopt the boys, their last names will be changed to Hogue. But what of their first names? I begin to pray about it, which leads me to a brilliant idea—why not just ask them? I start with the oldest, Justin. Oldest being a relative term, he's only seven. But he surprises me, as kids often do. "Daddy," he says, his voice serious, no smile, steady eye contact, "my old name makes me think of my old life. And this is a new life. So, yeah, I want a new name."

I want to be absolutely sure, so I tell him, "You'll have a new name, son. You'll be a Hogue, just like me."

"But I want a new first name." There is no playfulness in his voice, no petulance, either. He knows the importance of what I'm asking. And then, with just a hint of a smile, "And a new middle name, too, Daddy."

The first thought that comes to me is, why not give him my full name. Something else clamps over the thought, a dark cloud. No, if there's going to be a Junior in the house, it will be a biological son, my firstborn.

My firstborn.

The words shiver through me, but there it is. I pray about it, but since my mind is already decided, my prayers are little more than treading water, biding my time. Waiting for God to see it my way. There will be a Stephen James Hogue, Junior. He will be the flesh of my flesh, born of prayer and pleading, a miracle in my wife's womb. So be it.

A few days later, Jason Upton, a worship leader and singer-songwriter ministers at our church. I have always loved Jason's music, and as I take my seat, I'm greatly looking forward to what God is going to do with the service. Also, it will be nice to set aside my own dilemmas for a few hours, listen to someone else's story.

About halfway through the service, a feeling comes over me, sort of like God knocking on my skull. Pay attention, Stephen! Something is about to happen. And that's when Jason launches into the story of how he was adopted. His mother became pregnant at 19, and going against the advice of friends and family, who urged her to have an abortion, she decided to keep the baby. She named him Stephen. Young, confused, and without any support, she realized after a few months that her infant son deserved better. With much sorrow, she decided to give Stephen up for adoption. Before he left, though, she wrote him a letter, one that he could read upon becoming an adult. In it, she said that he would be a worshipper. She spoke over him the Psalms of David, she declared that he would love the Lord and live for Him.

Jason was 32 before he contacted the adoption agency, read the letter, discovering who his birth mother was. He looked her up, found that she's a devoted Christian, a part of her church's prayer and intercession team. He went to meet her. To his amazement, and hers also, she told him that she's been drawn to his music for years. And never knew the songs and beauty came from her own son!

Jason doesn't know me more than to say hello. He certainly isn't aware of the looming decision I'm to make. God told him to tell the story, he told it. And in the front row, I am a changed man. Stephen to Jason, Justin to Stephen. The clouds roll away, the sun comes out. What had I been thinking? Stephen James Hogue, waiting for me at home! I smile, I laugh. I'm at peace.

The next day, before I can talk with Justin, he comes in to talk with me. "Dad," he says, "I know what my name is going to be."

"Really?" I say. Well, this should be good. "So what's it going to be?"

He comes closer, takes my hand. "Daddy? What's your name?"

"Stephen."

"No, Daddy—your whole name. All of it."

"Stephen James Hogue."

His face lights up. "That's it! I want to be Stephen James Hogue!"

I hug him tightly and tell him I love him with all my

heart. I have prayed for so long and so fervently for a son of my own. And here he is. I just didn't see it. God's answers are never quite what we're looking for, and always more than enough.

Next, I need to decide on Daen's new name.

Daen is a very sweet, tender, and compassionate kid. He loves people and is always drawn to those who are hurting, doing his best to cheer them up. Whatever pain and harm he suffered as a young child, his heart was sheltered by God, for it is open to any who've experienced loss and need comforting. Seth is the name I come up with after praying. The name Seth means compensation, the ability to give to someone who has gone through loss and suffering.

Sitting with Daen, I tell him what the name means, how special it is. Seth was the child given to Adam and Eve after Cain killed Abel. Eve rejoiced when Seth was born because God had given her a child to replace the one she had lost. "That's who you are," I tell him. "You like to comfort people who've lost something. That's why God spoke to me about your new name." He stares up at me, his precious hazel eyes wide, listening to every word. "You're sweet and compassionate, you love to help those who've been hurt. You're a Seth."

Daen goes off, thinking about our conversation. He comes back a day or so later, and tells me he's ready to be Seth.

"When?" I ask.

He smiles like it's a trick question. "Now, of course."

And that's it. From that moment, the boys are Stephen and Seth. That's what they call themselves, that's what they tell others to call them. And they never slip, never make a mistake, never refer to each other by their old names. Truly, the old is gone, the new has arrived: Stephen and Seth.

* * *

One day, a week or so before the adoption hearing, I'm talking to Stephen, asking him how it feels. He's about as excited as a boy can get, and that's saying something. Then he says, "You'll be able to spank me, right?"

Not exactly the question I was expecting. "Well... yeah, I guess." And this amps him up even more, it's like Christmas, and he's just opened his best present ever. "You know what a spanking is, don't you, Stephen?"

He's beaming now, smiling circles into the air. "My old dad told us that if you ever spanked us, we should call 911 because you're not our real dad...only real dads can spank their kids. So once the judge says you're our one and only real dad, well..."

"I get to spank you," I finish. It's hard not to smile at his logic. "And you're right, I *could* spank you..." I pull him close, laughing, and hugging him. "But I won't. Hugs will have to do."

He smiles up at me. "That's okay, too."

A week later, the big day arrives. There is really nothing like it. Marriage comes closest, a forever ceremony, words that mean so much more than words can express. Because they are expressing something God-touched, and once spoken, nothing will ever be the same.

And they aren't. Quite literally, from that moment on, the boys' behavior changes. It's very much like they've been holding their breath for the whole two years, tense and hypervigilant, always looking over their shoulders, wondering when their father would reappear, take them back to a place they never wanted to go in the first place. And now, finally, something awesome and unimaginable has happened. They belong. It is no longer: this is the bed I sleep in, this is the place I put my clothes, these are my foster parents, but: This is *my* bed. This is *my* dresser. These are *my* parents.

This is my home.

Forever.

Stephen, Seth and their biological sister, Miranda.

Seth, Silas and Stephen.

Chapter Four

Sandra and Stephen

It is a rewarding and awesome duty God has granted us, the responsibility for our wondrous family. I feel blessed far beyond my worth. And certainly far beyond my abilities. Yet we function, and we function well. My children are growing in the Lord, they are strong and able, and better yet, they force me to be strong and able. For let's face it, they're kids—if I lose my connection with He who gives me my strength and ability, it's game over and lights out. Kids from foster care know far too much already about how mothers and fathers can fail them. What they need is to know that Sandra and I can provide them with what God has provided us—love, nurturing, discipline, and the unfailing belief that He's always available, always capable.

Was I this man when Sandra and I began dating in 1996? No. But truthfully, I'm not that man today. I keep striving, I keep learning. I fall down, and by God's grace, I get back up. If my children learn anything from me, I hope it's that—I fall down, I get back up. I have faith that a path is there, even though I can't see it.

Maybe that's what Sandra saw in me, this determination. It certainly wasn't money or status. The possibility of one day standing on a stage and preaching God's Good News about the plight of orphans seemed further away than one of God's hands from the other. Though now that I think of it, at the time we started dating in 1996, I *did* work at a church. And one could argue that the position I held was essential, the work I performed an absolute necessity.

I was the janitor.

In 1996, I'd recently lost a very well paying job, God's way of booting me into a new life. Along with a lack of employment, He also gave me a burning desire to more fully know Him, a deep inward need to rededicate my life to Him. So when the position of janitor at my church became available, I grabbed it. The five dollars an hour paycheck was a huge drop in salary, but I truly loved every minute of it. I loved vacuuming, sweeping, and preparing the church for use. I loved cleaning the toilets, setting up chairs and tables, and performing a hundred other tasks that people rarely notice unless they're left undone. It was a tremendous season of my life, one wherein I saw God in every chore, and in every detail.

And I guess He saw me, too, for one day, out of the blue, I received a phone call from the pastor of the church I'd attended while growing up. It had been four years since I'd seen him, yet, for some reason, God had put it in his heart that I should be their next youth pastor.

For a moment, holding the phone, I couldn't speak. Me, a youth pastor? I didn't have a college degree...

okay, let's get real here—I hadn't spent a single hour in a college classroom. I was a janitor, adept at cheerfully pushing a broom, making sure the toilet paper dispensers were always full, setting out chairs for the church services and taking them back in when the service was over. In what alternate reality did God see me as a youth pastor?

In a fit of wisdom, I asked my old pastor to give me some time to think about it. Then, fighting through the nervousness that always comes from asking advice, I went to see the senior pastor of the church I was attending and serving in my role as a janitor. I told him about the job offer to become a youth pastor, about how ill-equipped and unqualified I felt. I told him that my skill level was simply not adequate to the task, that my old pastor must have gotten me confused with someone more able. Then I did something wholly outside of my comfort zone—I asked him what he thought of me, and what I should do.

I remember the pastor leaning forward, locking eyes with me, smiling happily. He had an authority about him, a presence about him, a solidness that projected beyond his physical stature. "God is going to use you to do mighty things," he said to me. "Take the job, Stephen. Take it and step out into this next season. God has a special purpose in calling you. You're ready."

So I phoned the pastor who had offered me the job and said yes. As I spoke with him, it sounded like someone else's voice, deeper and more assured than mine. And maybe it was someone else. The person I was to become, the next season of my life.

Next on the list was Sandra.

"But I'm not called to be a pastor's wife."

These were Sandra's first words when I told her about the opportunity I'd been given. We were sitting in the parking lot of a Taco Bell after church on a Wednesday night. Okay, maybe I should have taken her someplace a little fancier. Or lacking the funds to do that, a place that had a fancier parking lot. True, we weren't married, but we were dating, which to Sandra meant that marriage wasn't far away. I did my best to achieve the same deep and assured voice I'd discovered in talking to the pastor. Apparently, God had used a ventriloquist for that conversation, for all I could feel was a sudden fear of losing Sandra. I explained that, really, this was good news. She explained that, really, she had friends who had received a special calling by the Lord to be a pastor's wife. And she wasn't one of them. I joked that maybe it was like call-waiting. Not even the hint of a smile.

We talked about it and talked about it, then we talked some more. The best I could come up with was the suggestion that not receiving a specific calling didn't mean she *wasn't* supposed to be a pastor's wife.

Eventually, Sandra warmed to the idea, but I doubt it was anything I said that changed her heart—when one has a heart as large as Sandra's, service, any service, comes naturally. In the end, I was her friend, I was chosen to serve—of course, she would help me. So, in January of 1997, I started as a full-time youth pastor at the New Covenant Assembly of God in Casselberry, Florida. And though we were still just dating, Sandra was right there with me, a dedication that had nothing to do with money, for I was paid little, and certainly not with position, for she had none, at least not officially. But the kids loved her, and she loved them, and most importantly, we greatly enjoyed working together.

More and more often, the thought came to me—this woman will be my wife. We will work together, bound by love, guided by God. We will have children, be a loving family, a shining example of Christ's light.

And I was right—in a way. Fall down, get back up. Again and again and again. The wonderful and difficult truth is, in order to teach a lesson, you first have to learn it.

Five

Selah

October, 2005

The people of the Dominican Republic are amazing, living in dire poverty yet still generous and welcoming, and our church mission trip there is a blessing to us as well as to them. Still, after nine days, I'm ready to come home, see how my wife and Silas and the two boys are doing.

From the Dominican Republic, it's a long trip home, but I'm happy to make it, happy to open the front door, walk up the stairs that lead to our second-floor section of the house. I set my bags down and look for Sandra... and discover a video camera on a tripod, a beaming, wide smile from Sandra.

"Welcome home. I have a gift for you!" Tears begin to seep from her eyes and flow down her cheeks. She hands me a gift bag filled with baby clothes. Before I can even process what's happening, she says, "You're going to be a father again!"

"A father? I'm... you're..." I say a quick prayer of gratitude, closing my eyes, doing my best to control my own tears. As I pull out the oversized baby girl clothes,

I'm confused, but still seem to utter, "You're pregnant? Really?"

"No... not exactly." The camcorder's light remains on, recording my every expression, joy to confusion, confusion to disappointment. My clothes are tacky from the trip, disheveled, I probably need a shave. I certainly need a shower. Not the best time to catch me on camera, but I pull myself straighter, rearrange my face. Whatever Sandra means, whatever God has in mind, it's good.

"I got a phone call," Sandra goes on, still filming me, her voice losing none of its excitement. "There's a baby girl who needs a home, a permanent home. She's only a few months younger than Silas. And we've been chosen!" When I just stand there, speechless, she says, "Honey—our Selah has finally arrived!"

Silas and Selah. Seven years before, God had whispered the names to us. Sandra would peel an onion, discover two onions inside. She'd crack open an egg, discover two yokes. People we hardly knew would come up to us, tell us we were going to have twins. We knew what the future held for us, we were absolutely sure of it—our first pregnancy would give us a boy and a girl.

There's a wise, old saying, one that we rarely quote except in hindsight—"Man plans, God laughs." Fifteen months after naming Silas and taking him home from the hospital, Sandra and I are told the second twin is on the way. Very funny, Lord. Very funny, indeed.

The nine-month old-girl brought to our home two days later is not named Selah, but from our first moments together, that's the name we anoint her with.

Selah, as used in the book of Psalms, means to 'stop and reflect' on the Word of God. It also has the powerful meaning of 'pause and worship'.

As usual, God's sense of humor is beyond me. I'm not even back into any routine, haven't spent quality time with my boys and the very next day, Selah is dropped off by the case worker. Instead of pause and worship, the air is filled with screaming and crying. I quickly leave the room, give Sandra some time to hold the girl, calm her down. Life has not been easy on her. Only nine months old, our home is already Selah's fourth placement and the first one without her older siblings.

After a few minutes, I go back into the living room. Selah again screams and cries. I leave, she calms down. I go in, she cries. This goes on all during the first day. And the second day. And the third. I start to think that perhaps the pause and worship isn't meant for her, but for me. Well, pause and worship is always a good idea, even if Selah's continuing aversion is hard on my ego. The screaming isn't about me, of course, I realize that—Selah absolutely abhors all men. Or perhaps a better way to say it is, she finds men absolutely frightening. It's difficult to imagine, she's only nine months old—but whatever happened to her, it wasn't good.

It takes a couple of weeks before the girl trusts enough to be comfortable with me in the room, and over a month before she'll let me hold her. For Selah, this is tremendous progress, and I'm proud of her. It's hard enough for adults to change—for a baby, lacking adult reasoning, lacking any real form of power, unable to say what it was she experienced, it's nothing short of miraculous.

And more good news—Silas and Selah get along fine together, this despite them being outwardly different as day is from night. First, there's size—six months younger than Silas, Selah outweighs her brother by nearly two to one. At nine months old, she wears the clothes of a child twice her age. And then there's food. Silas is a picky eater, we often struggle to get him to eat. That first night, their high chairs placed next to each other, Selah grabs every morsel she can reach, including a good deal of what's on Silas's plate. We think this is cute, we take pictures, her mouth stuffed to the brim, chubby cheeks pushing outward. Someday, we'll get out the scrapbook, sit around with our children and their husbands and wives, and laugh about it.

One day, Selah crams so much food in her mouth she almost chokes. Not so cute, and nothing to laugh at. We soon discover that the girl will eat anything. And I mean anything at all, including but not limited to blankets, sheets, clothes, pillows, items left on the ground, items left on low shelves, anywhere she can reach. At first, we assume she's just hungry. Really, really hungry. But it goes way beyond that. She has no 'off' button, she's continually in survival mode. She will literally eat until the food is pulled away—even if it's not food. Her mouth might say 'eech!', her stomach might say 'full', but her brain tells her to 'eat, eat, eat!'

Digging deeper into her history, we discover that Selah was neglected- often left alone, strapped into a car seat, or abandoned in her crib. Her mother was a drug-addicted prostitute. Procuring the next fix was always far more important than seeing to her baby's next meal. Somewhere in Selah's early development,

Silas and Selah in their high chairs.

the messages sent by her mouth and stomach were superseded by an overarching need to be filled. This need might have started with food, but by the time she arrives at our home, it goes far beyond it. She wasn't held, she wasn't nurtured, she wasn't nourished. Abandoned, powerless, hungry all the time, Selah knew only a hopeless emptiness. Her only way of shouting I will survive! was to reach for anything she could get her hands on and stuff it in her mouth.

Foster and adoptive parents tend to think that whatever the child lacked in the past, be it food, care, or love - once the supply is turned on by the new parents, the child will change. Sometimes this is true. Sometimes not. For abuse and neglect in a young child, and the child's reaction to them, are hard-wired into the brain. It doesn't matter that the child can't remember the abuse. The body remembers. The spirit remembers. Even before birth, while still in the womb, a child is captive to the mother's reality. Most people readily understand that if the mother ingests alcohol or drugs, those substances are passed on to the fetus. Less understood is that what the mother feels and thinks—towards herself, towards the baby, towards the life that lies outside—is also passed on. Just as the baby's body is formed in the womb, so is their emotional and mental roadmap of the world they are about to enter.

Selah has been deeply and repeatedly exposed to pain, hurt, rejection, abandonment, and a lack of love - exposed before she had any way to deal with it. God, in His infinite wisdom, has provided a cure—our family. This is what I remind myself every time she screams as I enter a room. Every time she screams as I pull something away from her mouth. Through His Son, God has given me all the love, patience, and power I need. Remember this, and Selah will eventually grow into the name chosen for her, a worshiper and bringer of worship. Forget it, and I'm as vulnerable to anger and frustration as any parent.

The problem is, as Selah grows older, her problems only intensify. She develops a terrible temper. She reacts poorly to even the simplest correction. For her first year and a half with us, I must also deal with Justin and Daen, who have severe attachment and behavioral problems of their own. But after the boys are adopted, after the Spirit of God has transformed them into Stephen and Seth, they change. Selah doesn't. Even though her adoption should have proceeded far more quickly and far more smoothly. Her two older siblings had already been slated for adoption when she came to live with us. The couple who was supposed to adopt them were simply unable to accommodate a third child. Unlike Stephen and Seth, who had to contend with the possibility of being returned to their father, Selah was ours from the start. So it should be easier.

But it isn't easier, because Selah isn't ours. In the eyes of the world, yes, absolutely—after six months, she's legally adopted, her name changed to Hogue, her place in our family made permanent. She's Selah Hogue when we take her to church, Selah Hogue when we register for her first day in school, Selah Hogue to anyone we meet in the supermarket or on the playground. Our child, our precious child, as though naturally born to us.

And yet, not ours, for a spiritual battle is being waged, with Selah as the battleground. True, from the greatest to the least, Satan leaves no one out of his plans. That said, he especially delights in tempting the weakest among us, those already made vulnerable. And Selah is vulnerable.

Anger and frustration are the devil's tools. No shortage of those qualities in Selah, that's for sure—or in me. And therein lies the real problem. Me. Ok, she doesn't like men, I get that. I'm gentle, I'm kind, I watch the tone of my voice, even the way I move. Despite these efforts, despite Sandra's efforts, Selah is almost always getting into some kind of trouble or another. She is willful, she disobeys, she throws tantrums whenever she doesn't get her way. Sometimes she throws tantrums even when she does get her way. With Selah, everything is a problem.

And it begins to wear on me. As the months tumble along, becoming years, her angry outbursts are more and more met by angry outbursts of my own. I try to remind myself that we said yes for a reason, but I feel the frustration bubbling through my veins, seeping into my heart. I don't understand this girl. No matter what discipline technique we use, no matter how many time-outs we give her, no matter what privileges we take away, or what rewards we offer, her behavior only worsens. With every new attempt at discipline, Selah grows more defiant, bolder, more arrogant in her disregard of rules. And I grow angrier and more frustrated. Who's training who?

One day, in the living room, thinking little about it, I ask Selah to go change her shirt to something that matches her shorts before we all go out to the store. A simple request, especially for the seven-year-old she's become. She responds by throwing herself to the floor, screaming at the top of her lungs, arms and legs thrashing like a bongo player gone berserk.

Selah at 7 years old.

"All I did was ask her to change her shirt!" I tell Sandra when she rushes in. She stares at me as though

I'm the one in need of discipline. Which is when it hits me—I am the one in need of discipline. Outwardly, of course, I've done nothing wrong. But my heart is boiling with ill-will. I don't want to discipline, I want to punish. I want to teach this girl a lesson once and for all. And it hits me—how often has God felt this way about me? How often has He said to me, I've shown you so many, many times? This time, please get it right!

"Go to your room," I tell Selah. "Go!" Despite the realization that, in God's eyes, my daughter and I have much in common, my voice still quivers with anger. While Sandra is seeing to the other three kids, I pace the floor, trying to compose myself. Trying to think of what I can do.

The answer that comes to me isn't a good one—there's nothing I can do. I've gone through every option I can think of, there's nothing left. Nothing at all. I close my eyes and cry out to God. It's impossible. "But not for you, Lord. For you, everything is possible. Please... guide me. Tell me what to do."

As I turn, walking towards Selah's room, I hear a gentle voice. The spirit of rejection is upon Selah.

The spirit of rejection. Four simple words, but it's as if my mind opens, I see all, scene after scene—left alone in the car seat, abandoned in her crib, nothing to eat, no one to hold her, no one to answer her cries, no one to show her love, parental rights voluntarily surrendered. Every time I correct her, that's all Selah feels, all she sees. Rejected even before that. Rejected in the womb by a mother who didn't want her, who saw her only as a mistake, a problem. Then moved from house to house, foster family to foster family, the feeling of rejection growing. And finally separated from the only beings she loved, her older siblings, who got to stay in a home while she was moved to another. Why didn't that parent want her, too?

Whatever the reason, it was nothing a young child could understand. No wonder she gets so upset and defiant. The spirit of rejection has her by the throat, choking her—all she's doing is fighting back.

It comes to me that for years now, all I've been doing is treating her behavior. We've tried a number of approaches, listened to several different experts, done our best to apply their techniques. All by the book, to be sure. But not by The Book. The problem, I suddenly realize, isn't how to change her behavior, but the far more serious problem of how to wrest her from darkness into light.

Feeling very much like God whacking me on the back of the head, it hits me that I know what to do. I turn on some worship music, letting the words and tones change the atmosphere. Once I'm calm and centered, I go to our pantry, take down the olive oil. Only then do I go to Selah's room. I ask her to sit on the bed, and once she has, I kneel opposite her, looking into her eyes. No anger in me now, only the confidence that comes from communion with God. I say to Selah, "Sweetheart, I know that I'm looking into your eyes, but listen—I'm not speaking to my sweet little girl. Ok?"

I let a moment pass, then I say, "Satan, by the power of Jesus Christ, you cannot have my daughter! Loose your grip over her life now. I am her father, she is my daughter. She is not yours, she is a child of God, and you cannot have her!" I take in a deep breath, focus myself on the indwelling Lord. "Spirit of rejection, loose your grip over my daughter! She has not been rejected, she is accepted and loved and cherished. She is valuable and special, and God has a plan and a purpose for her life that you cannot destroy. You hear me? You cannot destroy my wonderful girl or the wonderful plans God has for her! She will no longer believe your lies. She will always love God and serve Him and live for Him and be confident that His love will never leave her, never abandon her. Never!"

I take the oil and anoint Selah's forehead, praying over her and speaking into her life. Then I simply hold her for a long time. There is no anger in my girl or in me, there is only love—my love, surely, but also a much greater love. I feel it, Selah feels it. So I just hold her, letting both of us bask in His love, His acceptance. A love and acceptance given freely.

On this day, everything changes for Selah. As it does for me. Unless you change and become like little children, you shall not enter the kingdom of heaven. Children listen to their Father. In this, I am as much a child as Selah. There is only one answer. On this day, Selah truly enters our family, not because I have been told the answer, but because I have at last remembered to ask the question.

* * *

There is another part of Selah. The part that is to become a worshiper and a bringer of worship. And that is perhaps why the battle for her spirit has been so fierce. From the time she arrives—well, at least from the time she stops screaming whenever I enter the room—the Lord has told me to pray over her throat, for Selah will have the voice of an angel. My prayer has always been for her to sing songs that reflect heaven and praise God. Sandra and I know almost nothing of her genetic background, whether she comes from a long line of opera stars or whether her previous family tended more towards tone-deaf bar-bellowers. Nor does it matter. God is great—if she is meant to sing, then sing she will.

And sing she does. As the months and years go by, even as she becomes more and more disobedient, the song in her remains. Not a harsh sound, but sweet; nothing strident or reflective of her fear and anger, but cheerful notes, the contented warbling of a songbird. It's as though, however much Satan tries, he cannot touch this God-given gift, cannot pervert it, or use it, or take it away. When she sings, Selah is a joyous child.

She's been with us for over three years when one Sunday a lady in the choir at our church walks up to Selah with a message. "God is going to give you many songs," she tells my daughter. She then hands Selah a notepad emblazoned with a musical note. "Write them down." The lady smiles.

It is difficult to predict how Selah will react to strangers, especially strangers that give her gifts. So I watch her closely. But all Selah does is take the notepad, staring at it. Then she looks up, reflecting a smile back at the lady. She's only four, of course—she doesn't know how to write, either words or musical notations. But all that day, she treasures the notepad, keeping it close to her, and that's enough. One day, perhaps she'll dig it out of whatever drawer she's left it in and write something. Who knows?

As usual, I have the timing a little off. The very next day, Selah runs up to me, hands me the notepad, placing a pen between my fingers. "Daddy! I have a song! You write it down for me." She then sings me the sweetest little song, which I copy down line by line.

This happens again and again over the next few years. However loud she gets when I tell her to clean up her room, however much she thumps and pounds floors and walls to get her way, I find it impossible to forget the sound of her singing just an hour before.

One day, Selah comes into my office and very seriously asks me to teach her how to play the piano. So we go into the music room, where I sit her down at our piano, explaining a few basics about the keys, keeping it simple. After all, she's only seven. I then teach her four basic chords, telling her that these chords can be used to play a great variety of worship songs. Using the chords, I show her how to play one of them. Then I leave. We usually don't let the kids play the piano without supervision, but I think, how much harm can she do?

Ten minutes later, I hear the piano, I hear Selah singing. At first, I think someone else must be in with her, for the song is played perfectly. The words, also, are right on key. So I look in, see only Selah. I glance about, checking the corners. No one. Just Selah, playing as well as I can. It's the Lord, of course, once again knocking me on the head, saying, I don't ask you to pray so you can feel good about praying—I ask you to pray so that I can answer.

Selah's problems aren't over, not by a long shot.

We all fall down, we all learn to get back up. But even though the battles continue, the war has already been won. She knows now to Whom she sings. And that's a lesson of a lifetime.

Selah's Adoption Day.

Chapter Six

Sandra and Stephen

Like any large family, Sandra and I have a busy schedule, doubly so now that God has given me an orphan's ministry. I stand on church stages all across this country, sharing God's love for the orphan, the foster child, the throwaway child. These are the children Jesus talks about when he says, Come to me—needy hearts in small bodies, children whose behavior and actions often drive away the very care they crave. Come to me. It sounds so simple. Pull a child out of a horrible situation, place the child with people who have hearts filled with love, and are willing to share it. The child should be joyous and grateful.

It rarely works out that way. Not quickly, at least. Because it's rarely just about the foster child. Sure, they have much to learn from us, and we have much to teach them and give them. Keep it on that level, and failure is pretty much inevitable. For there's also the vast unknown of what we need to learn from them.

In this, adoption is very similar to marriage. God put Sandra and me together, but the rest was—and always will be—up to us. It's as though He's saying, "Here are a couple of talents and kids—let's see what you can do with them." We struggle to be faithful to His gifts, to learn and grow and use what He's given us in the best possible way. And invariably, we fail. Because there are no perfect marriages. No perfect parents, either. And certainly, no perfect kids. There are only those of us who strive to listen and learn, who stumble and fall and then make corrections, brush off our pants, and continue on towards the light. Because the alternative is to give up, take a seat on the sidelines and watch the parade go by.

Truthfully, I wish I didn't stumble so often. Or lacking that, perhaps learn how to end it with a graceful flourish, a little Ta-Da! at the end of the fall to convince everyone that I had it under control all the while. At heart, I don't want to look like a fool. Who does?

When I was dating Sandra, and even after we were married, I didn't like to make choices, because I didn't want people, especially Sandra, to see how often I chose poorly. To disguise this, I put on a cloak of happy-go-lucky, a nothing-can-get-me-down attitude that I wore as both shield and armor. Whatever came my way, I put a positive spin on it. Don't get me wrong, positive is a good thing—but not when it's used to hide from the mistakes we all make. Or even worse, to hide from the mistakes we didn't make because we weren't brave enough to step out and take a chance.

Before getting married, Sandra and I signed up for pre-marriage counseling, where we were asked to take several personality tests. My favorite was the animal test—a battery of questions which revealed whether the test-taker was a lion, a golden retriever, an otter, or a beaver. The lion was a leader, bold, and confident; the golden retriever was loyal, kind, and sensitive, the beaver organized and prepared. And then there was my personal favorite, the otter, Mister laid-back, a fun-loving being that no amount of adversity could overcome.

Never for a moment did I doubt where the test would place me. In fact, I scored a perfect 40 for Otter, and absolutely nothing in all the other animal categories. That's nothing, as in zero, zilch, not a one. I wanted to shout for joy when I got the results—a perfect score! God must have really been on His game when he picked me to walk down the aisle with Sandra. The oldest of four in a family without a father in the house, she was overly concerned with details, with practicalities, with getting things done. She most definitely needed an Otter in her life, a little fun to go with the drudgery, a bit of care-free to balance her level-headed, pragmatic approach. How could this be anything but a good idea?

If I'd only cocked an ear and listened, I probably would have heard a host of angels break into uproarious laughter. But I didn't listen. I plunged ahead, happy and oblivious. Go, otters!

Stephen, Selah, Seth and Silas.

In the summer of 1997, on a beautiful, sunny day, surrounded by about three hundred friends and family, Sandra and I were married. Afterward, I wandered about the grounds with a dizzy smile glued to my face, radiant with gratitude, the presence of God so thick around me that I couldn't take a breath without feeling His love and warmth pulsing through every cell. Which was when a man I'd known all my life came over to me, his eyes shimmering with light as he wrapped an arm around my shoulder. "Don't worry," he said, breathing in the wonderful air, "Your marriage will get better."

For a moment, I was too stunned to talk. I wanted to tell him that Sandra and I were fine, we were great, we were totally in love—but he beat me to it. "Sure, it all seems perfect now. Problem is, young man, perfect doesn't last. Your marriage will be tested, and then it will be tested some more. Some of the tests, you'll barely make it out the other end. But you will make it. As long as you cling to God, the tests will only strengthen your love. Strengthen your wife. Strengthen your marriage." He turned to me, flashing a wide grin, and gave me a playful slap on the back. "It's going to be great!"

As he walked away, I wanted to shout after him, It already is great! Instead, I hurried back to find Sandra, making sure she hadn't disappeared.

The problems began almost immediately. Being positive is a fine trait. But like all fine traits, when taken to an extreme, it becomes a weakness. I didn't like to make decisions, because I was afraid of being wrong. Of course, this wasn't exactly what I told myself. Ok, it wasn't anywhere near what I told myself. Instead, I took the easy way out, rationalizing about how I was mature enough to let Sandra make her own decisions. And decisions for us. Along with her own decisions, of course, she would make her own mistakes. Only natural. And I would comfort her, because, hey, that's what a good husband does.

The day after we returned from our honeymoon, Sandra began her master's program at the University of Central Florida. I went back to work as a youth pastor, making very little money. I figured we'd just go with the flow, trust in God until something better came along. This wasn't necessarily a bad approach—however, there's a difference between faith and timidity. I didn't pray with my wife, didn't hold hands with her and ask the Lord of my life for what I truly wanted, because what if He didn't give it to me? No way to view that as anything but a failure. Nor did I take charge of our finances. I figured Sandra was better with numbers. It made sense to let her take on that responsibility. The truth was, I did little to steer our marriage one way or the other. "Trust in God," I was fond of saying, "and everything else will work itself out."

Now trust in God is a marvelous thing. However, using a patina of trust to avoid our God-given responsibilities is not. God doesn't ask Man to lead because he's better or smarter or even stronger than Woman—no, he's given this task because leadership involves sacrifice. It involves unwavering commitment. It involves the willingness, in one form or another, to lay down one's life. I wasn't showing faith when I said trust God, everything will work itself out. I was simply letting events make my decisions for me, thus avoiding responsibility and blame.

When Sandra complained about my role, it wasn't about trusting God, she trusted God just fine—it was me she had doubts about. And with good reason. By entering into the sacrament of marriage, I was called to protect Sandra. In Christ, I was to be the rock on which life's tempests crashed down upon. Sandra and the children were the vessels of life kept safe in the harbor I protected.

Sandra was and is a strong woman, a take-charge personality with a God-given capacity to lead. So, in the first few years of our marriage, when I shunned leadership, when I failed to protect, she had no choice but to take my place. And she resented me for it. She resented me not making decisions, not risking the possibility of a mistake. And I resented her for showing me my weaknesses.

God disciplines those he loves. The root of discipline is to teach. But a teacher needs a student, and I wasn't so interested in learning. Not this lesson, at least. It made me uncomfortable. It made the easy road I'd chosen seem less than courageous. Still, as the problem became more and more evident, I began to study on it. Maybe it didn't show outwardly, but inwardly, the walls I had built to protect myself—which in truth only diminished me—those walls, if not fallen yet, were crumbling.

God's timing is always perfect, so it was during this vulnerable period of my life when Sandra said something that completely tore me apart. It was a Wednesday, just after I'd finished preaching our youth service. We found ourselves off in a corner, alone for the first time that day. Sandra has a dazzling smile and taking my hand, she unleashed the full force of it. "You should hear yourself. When you preach, you're a lion of God, you radiate the Holy Spirit."

I smiled. Ok, I beamed. Who wouldn't? My mouth opened—Sandra quickly put a finger to my lips. She wasn't finished. Her smile didn't diminish, but her eyes dimmed, a sadness welling up behind them. "But as soon as you step away from the podium, the lion flees. I go home with a passive lamb."

Being who I am, I did my best to spin this into a positive. Lamb? Ok, that might be good. Lamb of God, the song of the lamb. Next came passive—I admit, not a word one usually wants to be attached to their name. Still, it had possibilities. Gandi, Martin Luther King Junior, passive resistance. I wanted to argue but saw immediately that it was useless. Not because she was argumentative, but because she was truthful. In my wife's eyes, I had become little. Worse still, there was no one to blame but myself. In life, it is impossible to stand still. By choosing not to grow, I had chosen to shrink. I had made myself little.

A few days later, Sandra and I were discussing our need to buy a new computer. Sandra quoted numbers, saying that we really couldn't afford one. I said not to worry, the computer was needed to help in our ministry, God would surely honor us. At this, Sandra simply smiled, the tolerant but wearied look a teacher gives to a somewhat dim student. Our married life had taught her that she was the one who made the financial decisions, so she patiently repeated the numbers, telling me once again that we couldn't afford it.

Which is when something clicked in my slow-working brain. I saw it all very clearly. If I gave in, as I was about to, I could blame Sandra for any coming failures in my ministry. I wouldn't even have to mention it. The thought would always be there—if only we'd had that new computer...

Is that who I was? Really? More importantly, is that who God wanted me to be?

"No, honey," I said. "We need the computer."

The argument intensified. In her thinking, Sandra was right, of course. We couldn't afford a new computer. There was ample reason for me to give in without losing face. But I didn't. It wasn't that I resented her for calling me a passive little lamb. One can be hurt by the truth, but how can one resent it? No, this was something else. I was finally getting it. By taking the weight of the decision on my shoulders, I was protecting her. If I was right, I would praise God, praise Sandra for supporting me. If I was wrong, there would be only me to blame. My decision, my responsibility.

"Sandra..." I took her hand, I looked into her eyes. Sandra's eyes are usually dark pools brimming with love and life... but they can also be fiery volcanoes, dangerous to approach. "Sandra, the discussion is over. I've made my decision, there's no need to talk about it any further."

The voice I spoke with was calm, assured... which surprised me, for my heart was telling me it wanted to rip my chest apart and make a run for it, start life over someplace safer. Sandra was going to kill me!

To my amazement, a smile bright as dawn rose on her lips. "Ok," she said. "If that's what you want."

Ok? Ok? Without a doubt, I knew Sandra disagreed

with my decision. And yet, and yet... I studied her. No doubt about it, the smile was real.

Your marriage will be tested, I heard the man say. But if you cling to God...

Cling to God. Cling to His holy words. It seemed like such a small decision, buying a computer. But if I couldn't learn to lead in the small things, how would I ever lead in the truly important decisions? It wasn't about brow-beating my wife into seeing it my way, it certainly wasn't about bully-domination. Jesus gives us the model of a leader—meek and yet unwavering in his dedication to the truth, urging us on not by the sting of his whip but by the light of his example, serving and giving without complaint, laying down his life so that others might gain life.

And if I didn't lead? If I refused the role God had assigned me? Easier that way, less conflict, less blame, less danger. The man who buried his Talent in Matthew 25 must have felt like that—safe, no risk of investing and losing, no record of unwise choices. Some might even call that wisdom.

Like all men, I am hardly perfect. On my own, I'm not only an imperfect leader, but I'm also often not a leader at all. But I have come to realize this—I am a child of God, a son, not a slave, and I love the confidence He has in me. Confidence to lead my wife, to lead my family, to show the world a loving example. This is the man my wife delights in following, not the perfect man, for there is no perfect man but the one God sent down to us.

Have I succeeded in this quest? Have I learned how to lead? If I would ask that, I would be asking the wrong question. Babies learn to walk by falling down, kids topple off bicycles before they get it right. Learning is a lifelong endeavor. The most I can say is that I'm getting better at getting back up, brushing the dust off my pants and cheerfully continuing on. I can do this because I know where I'm going, even if I don't always know the way. Follow Him who calls to me, and I can't go wrong. More than that, follow Him, and I can have confidence that the ones who follow me are in safe hands. And that's all I want.

Our family picture.

Christmas 2010.

Chapter Seven

Life as a Foster Parent

Fall, 2006

I'm readying myself for the day's coming work, staring into the bathroom mirror as I shave, my only prayer being 'Please, Lord, this time, no cuts' when a name forms in my mind. *Siloam.* I recognize it from the Gospel of John, where Jesus heals a blind man by making some mud, putting it on the blind man's eyes, then telling the man to wash in the pool of Siloam. The name means *Sent*.

In a little over two years, we've gone from no children to three boys and a girl—but Sandra wants one more, another girl, a newborn this time, and she's been bombarding heaven with her plea. And God has heard! This is what the name means, I have no doubt at all. Siloam!

I'm so excited that I forget my half-shaven face and hurry to find Sandra. "God gave me the name of the baby girl He's sending!"

If Sandra is surprised, she doesn't show it. Instead, she flashes me a smile, her grin almost mischievous.

"He gave me a name, too." Then she holds up a hand. "On three?"

Ok, this probably sounds ridiculous, but we've done it before, more than once, usually for the amount to give in an offering. Amazingly, we almost always come up with the same number. Only this time, it's not a number we're looking for, it's a name. And hardly a common one, either.

"One," she says. "Two... three!"

In perfect unison, we both shout, "Siloam!" I stare at my wife. She stares at me. Then we both began to cry and laugh at the same time. The girl will be a newborn, I'm sure of it. Maybe even a newborn from Sandra's womb. Siloam. Sent. On her way.

In the coming months, Sandra buys a crib, pink and purple butterflies and flowers on the trim, matching mobile to hang above, matching crib skirt, the whole nine yards. It's an expense we can barely afford, but setting it up in Selah's room, it seems perfect. Over the years, we've continued to see a fertility doctor, but for the first time in a long while, there's a renewed sense of hope. Or maybe the foster agency will call. Sandra's gone so far as to add a special foster agency ring tone to our phone, the sound of a siren.

In the weeks that come, we get into the habit of going into Selah's room, standing by the crib, playing with the baubles hanging down. We talk about what it will be like, having another girl. Sometimes Selah joins us. She's going to love having a little sister, someone to protect and nurture the way she was never protected or nurtured. Someone she can sing to sleep. Also, five children in a home is the legal limit of the state's foster care system. Not five foster children, but five children of any type- natural, adopted, or foster. So it'll be perfect—three boys, two girls. Absolutely perfect.

There's only one small problem—months go by, Sandra doesn't get pregnant. More months go by. The phone doesn't ring, at least not with a child who will be staying forever.

Still, there is much to be grateful for. My job at Calvary Christian Center is going well. I've now been there for six years. People know me, know my family. And then there's the adoption of Stephen and Seth, a truly glorious day. After the judge bangs down his gavel, after he tells Sandra and I that "you are the parents of these boys, as though naturally born to you", after he says to the boys, "Say hello to your mom and dad, kids", after the cheering and the picture-taking, members of the church host a party for us. Cake, pizza, big banner, the whole shebang. We are honored that even though we are the only ones fostering and adopting in our church congregation, they understand the magnitude- both in the physical and spiritual realm.

The crib in the corner of Selah's room isn't exactly forgotten, but other issues crowd around it. Silas's growth rate is less than it should be, we'll need to find a specialist. Selah continues to overeat and overreact, her behavior ranging from incendiary to explosive. Not to mention that after ten years of marriage, I'm still on the upward learning curve of becoming a godly leader.

But all families have problems. I can deal with that. And all husbands and fathers struggle to be godly—to be the perfect reflection of our Father is an ongoing and lifelong quest.

Often, I'll be loading the kids into the van...one, two, three, four... and I turn around for the next one. It's a deer-in-the-headlights moment for me, this sensation of another couple seats needing to be filled. That despite my count, I've misplaced a kid or two. I can almost see them, shadows dancing and laughing just out of my sight. I stick my head back in the van, count the kids again, just to be sure—Silas, Selah, Seth and Stephen, all in their seats.

Then I notice Sandra's face—I can actually see the numbers form on her lips, one, two, three, four, her face wearing the same quizzical expression I would see if I looked in a mirror. Our eyes meet, our confusion twinning into understanding, a warmth that flows from her heart to mine and back again, the surety that God isn't done with us yet. We *are* missing a kid or two. We just haven't been introduced to them yet.

Problem is, in the foster care system, foster parents never know when a call will come, or who that call will bring into their home. A teacher, a neighbor, a relative suspects abuse, and reports it to the authorities. If warranted, a child welfare worker will investigate the report. Investigators don't work an eight to five job, for the simple reason that child abuse isn't confined to normal working hours. Bars close, users run out of drugs, a parent gets fired, evicted, a spouse leaves, or cheats... the reasons used to justify child abuse are legion. So we might get a call late at night, early in the morning, on the weekend... anytime. Since investigators are strictly limited in the hours they can keep a child with them, a foster home must be found and found quickly.

Nor is there a set type of victim. Newborns suffer, so do teenagers; boys suffer, so do girls. It's an epidemic that crosses all socio-economic boundaries, visiting blacks, whites, Hispanics, rich kids, and poor. And while foster parents have a right to say yes or no to the child placement agency, it's a right we've set aside. Whoever the child, whatever the circumstances, Sandra and I have already decided—we will say yes.

Sometimes we're told about the details of the child's former home, given some idea of how long the child will stay with us, if there's a possibility of adoption. More often, we're told almost nothing. Sometimes this is because the case worker doesn't know these things, and therefore can't tell us. Whatever the reason, it can be frustrating. But then, all parenting can be frustrating. Sandra and I have developed a little trick—whatever the story, we act as if the child will be staying forever. Actually, it's less of a trick and more of a prayer. We pray for the biological family to know Jesus and get healing. And if they don't, we pray that we can keep them and love them and give them a forever home, a home that will hold their hearts and always welcome them back.

But something strange happens. As the year turns into two years, as two years turn into three. The siren sounds, again and again. The case worker tells us there's a child in need, the parents are drug addicts, or in jail, or in treatment, or can't be found. We always say the same thing—bring them over, our home is their home.

It occurs to me that perhaps the shadows I see while loading kids into the van aren't the children God is bringing us, but the ones He's taking away—because no matter how much we love them, no matter how great the improvement in their behavior and trust and general enjoyment of life, they all leave. The case worker calls, tells us to have the child ready on whatever hour and day has been decided. We do our best to reassure the child, focusing on the photos and artwork covering our refrigerator and adorning our walls, how we'll love them, pray for them and remember them forever. We pack their belongings, and on the appointed day, help them out to the case worker's car. We smile and wave goodbye, tears in our eyes.

I do my best to hide my emotions, but seeing a child go feels like someone ripping my chest open and tearing out my heart. Still, a strong front is needed, because however much it affects me, I can see that it's even harder on Sandra. For a week or so after a child leaves us, her heart, usually so inclusive and joyous, is bruised and tender and in need of shelter. And what of our children? Perhaps it's hardest of all on them, for they share their bedrooms, their toys, their parents, their lives. The question in their eyes when a child leaves is both obvious and brutal—*why did we get to stay, when others have to leave?* I give them honest answers. But their young minds don't quite understand sometimes.

Our latest charges are two cousins, Mindy, a lovely wisp of a light-haired, fair-skinned girl, round brown eyes, and Audrey, the older of the two, blue-eyes, darkish blond hair. They are cousins from two different states, joined together in FL, and removed together because the adults who were supposed to take care of them were arrested for the sale and use of illegal drugs. We think and hope and pray that the girls have found their forever home, and for a long while, our hope seems to have a foundation. But then, after nearly two years, in the space of two months, both girls are taken away.

First to go is Mindy. Someone from the foster care agency calls, tells us that a sister of Mindy's dad is willing to care for the girl. Since Audrey isn't related to that side of the family, she has to stay. *How long before Mindy leaves?* we ask. We're told that the aunt is flying down from Ohio in a week.

Seven days. Not much time. Or perhaps too much time. This is Mindy's home, and Audrey is more sister than a cousin. Doubt and fear assailed them both. Is getting sent away a punishment? Or is it a blessing? We tell Mindy that someone wants her and loves her, that she'll get to live with her aunt and cousins. But isn't Audrey a cousin? Why can't she go, too? We do our best to explain how Mindy's aunt isn't Audrey's aunt, we wrap our arms around Audrey and say that we love her very much and are so glad she's staying. Which only makes Mindy want to stay, too. It's an impossible situation.

A week later, Mindy's aunt arrives, and after spending a short while with her, trying to cram nearly two years of experience and observations into a few days. Then, they drive away. We wave until they are out of sight, smiles plastered on our faces. We have photos, of course, but who needs photos when the memories are like hot coals seared into our consciousness. Nearly two years—how do we not remember Mindy's squeaky voice, how do we not see the cute way she tilted her head whenever she asked a question? And what about Audrey? For most of Audrey's life, Mindy has been her companion, the one constant in an ever-changing world.

A short two months later, the same case worker calls—Audrey's mother is out of jail, has completed her requirements, and Audrey will be leaving. "How long?" we ask, sounding like a broken record. Only days this time. I turn to the precious girl, stroke her hair—she's been with us for 22 months, 2 weeks and 3 days, not that anyone's counting.

Two days later, when the case worker comes to escort Audrey to her new home, all the children walk out the door with her, carrying her toys, her bags, her books. They walk with heads down, silent—like a funeral procession. Then, as Seth hands her a big Teddy bear, he begins to cry. We all join him, though I, the rock that I am, do my best to hide it.

I remember years before, the case worker having to pull Seth from the car, yelling and screaming and crying. I thought that was horrible. Turns out I was wrong—*this* is horrible. My kids would hold onto Audrey forever if they could. Who knows better how she feels, dragged once again into the fear and uncertainty of a new home, new school, new life? It's all too much. I watch her tear-streaked face press against the car window, a small hand limply waving goodbye as the car starts up, drives away. Too much.

After the car turns a corner, disappearing, we all slowly wander back into the house. I gather the family together for prayer. "Lord," I say, "help Audrey remember God's love and the love we will always have for her. And help us remember the love she's given us. For we've been blessed to know Audrey, to know what a beautiful child of God she is. And that's a forever thing, Lord. Wherever she is, whatever type of problems she's having, remind her that You are always with her. You will watch over her."

Still, it hurts. I see it in the others, I feel it in myself, like a deep bruise, one that doesn't show on the outside, but which stabs deeply when we move in the wrong way. For days afterward, we tiptoe around, trying not to wake the memories.

Then, before I'm at all ready, the siren again sounds. Sandra and I are sitting in the living room—neither of us jumps to answer it. Perhaps, just this once, we can let it go to voice mail. The thought makes me uncomfortable, as though it's God Himself calling, as though I'm saying, *Hey, enough's enough already, Lord. Let someone else take the weight.* In a way, it is God calling, for some child of His creation needs help, and if I'm not saying *Here I am, Lord*, then what am I saying?

Less quickly than I ought, I reach for the phone, listening to the caller. I whisper to Sandra, "A boy. Nine months old." She gives me a nod and a half-smile. Sandra loves kids, especially the babies! "Sure," I say. "Bring him over." A short while later, the case worker arrives with a child asleep in his car seat. The diaper bag accompanying him is full of dirty, mismatched clothes. And girl's clothes to boot. We immediately toss them in the trash, trying not to be disappointed in whoever's been providing care.

The child's name is Johnson. In truth, Johnson makes any feeling of disappointment impossible. Even poorly dressed, he's one of the cutest, most appealing children I've ever met, a blue-eyed, blond-haired bundle of joy. He can't yet talk, but the burbling melodies that come out of him sound like doves cooing. His smile is entrancing, his eyes lively and inclusive, his pudgy hands always reaching out for a hug. We call him Jo-Jo, I think because there's so much gladness in him, so much glee, you just have to say his name twice. Jo-Jo. Just like you have to go over to him, pick him up, cuddle the little guy. He's so very easy to love.

We ask the agency for more information on Johnson. They give us a video link to a local TV news broadcast, a clip showing people being arrested at a meth lab, herded into a black van. One of those arrested is a pregnant woman. Johnson's mother. Since she gave birth in jail, her newborn son was immediately placed in foster care. Though the foster agency never says as much, I'm thinking, the mom's in jail, Jo-Jo's never even really met her—our fifth child, for sure!

As the months pass, we are delighted to see Jo-Jo take his first steps, speak his first words. My father, especially, becomes close to the boy. My mother is not well, we know that her spirit will soon be called home. A blessing for Mom, but a grievous loss for those who cherish her. More and more, my father seems to find comfort in Jo-Jo, holding him, cuddling him, letting the wonder and life of the boy assure him that even when the people closest to us die, love remains.

Then Johnson's mother gets out of jail. I don't know what to expect, but from all I've seen and experienced, only problems can come of it.

In this expectation, I'm dead wrong. Most parents who've had children removed and placed into foster care view the foster parents as the enemy. We have their kids. We *stole* their kids. It isn't right, it isn't fair, because however they've treated their children, they're the parents, they had their reasons, it's their call. But Johnson's mother turns out to be as special as her son. She knows she needs to learn, she wants to work with us, to listen to any advice we have for her. More than anything else, she wants to be a good mother, to do whatever it takes to get her son back.

We send her photos, she writes us letters, she talks with Johnson over the phone. Slowly, she gets to know her son, eventually earning the privilege of visiting with him. It's impossible not to admire her hard work, her desire to change her life; impossible not to help her, to love her for so wanting to love her child. At the same time, in my most secret heart, I have trouble saying *her child*. He's not her child—he's *our* child. However much she changes, she'll never be able to give Jo-Jo as good a life as we can. A mother, a father, a sister, brothers, extended family, a church family. Never.

The problem is, my most secret heart is no secret to God. Like a guilty child, I can feel His disappointment. Repent, Paul tells us, and prove your repentance with deeds. And I do. Daily, sometimes hourly, I find myself repenting of evil thoughts—thoughts of putting my needs first, my happiness before others. Sandra and I work hard to help Jo-Jo's mother—this is the proof of my repentance. I pray for the woman, I earnestly scour my heart of any feelings but the wonder of God raising up one of His fallen children, giving her a hope and a future.

In getting to know Johnson's mother, we come to realize this—hope and a future, sure. But experience? She's a mother in name only, lacking even a single day of on-the-job training with the boy whom I can't help but think of as our son. If we needed a babysitter, she wouldn't be my first choice. Nor my second. Nor third. Officially, teaching the biological mom parenting skills is not our responsibility. It's left up to the professionals in the child welfare system.

Problem is, Sandra and I are the ones raising Jo-Jo. Sandra and I are the ones who know his behaviors. Sandra and I are the ones best suited to convey this information. Or, I should say, Sandra is. If Jo-Jo had a father, I would be the one talking to him. But he has only a mother, so the task of teaching falls to my wife. They talk on the phone, they meet at the agency building, discussing discipline techniques, the foods Jo-Jo likes, his daily routine, how a mother can stay loving even when she's tired, angry, distracted.

Through it all, Sandra remains upbeat, but I can see that it's wearing her down. Wearing me down, too. Mindy, Audrey, so many others. And now, Jo-Jo. Good outcomes, I tell myself. The goal of foster care is reunification. These are happy stories, stories of parents trying to better themselves, stories of relatives willing to step in. I should be overjoyed.

But I'm not. It's now been nearly five years since the name Siloam came to me. Five long years. I'm the leader of this family—have I done something wrong? Have I somehow been found lacking in my zeal? My wife hides her sorrow well, but she is hurting, and there seems nothing I can do to help her. Nothing.

"School starts next week," Sandra calls to me one morning. "I'm taking the gang to the beach. Want to come?"

I'm tempted, but... "No," I tell her. "I need to work on my Orphans message." And to myself, *I need to pray. I need some answers.* So I help Sandra load the van, wave as they drive away. Then go back into the house.

But I get nothing done. The quiet, instead of focusing me, has become a distraction. I rise and stretch, then wander from room to room, finally stopping at Jo-Jo's bed. Two teddy bears and a lumpy manatee sit on the pillow. Lumpy because the boy hugs it so tightly at night. I try to imagine the bed vacant, but I can't. A silly thought comes to me—maybe I can hide the manatee, put it back in the bed after Jo-Jo is gone. Next, I wander into Selah's room, into the corner where we've placed the crib. Dust has gathered on the mobile hanging above it. I find a rag, wipe it clean, wipe the butterflies and flowers till they gleam. Sandra and I have faith. A name was given, a baby will come. I bow my head, tears in my eyes. "Please, Lord..."

But that's as far as I get before I hear the Lord nudge me and say, "Do you trust Me?" I go back to my office realizing it won't be long before my family comes home and I won't get anything else done.

A short two hours later, I am startled by the loud noise of the front door slamming open. The house abruptly filled with a whirlwind of noise, five kids rushing in, Sandra saying something, her voice lost in the commotion.

"Daaaaad! I can't fit the cooler in the closet!"

Before I can take two steps, Sandra rushes in. "They found a baby for us! A newborn!" And when my mouth does nothing other than fall open, "They called while we were at the beach. That's why we came back."

My mind is a swirl of questions. The state only allows five kids—with our four plus Jo-Jo, we're not allowed another. And a newborn at that—many homes would love a newborn. Why are we being chosen?

"Her name is Fabianna," Sandra tells me, the hope evident on her face. "Her mother's got a drug problem, the baby was born addicted."

"But shouldn't she be in the Neonatal Intensive Care Unit?"

Sandra shrugs. "There's really nothing to be done but see her through withdrawal. We can do that here. Plus, the poor baby's barely five pounds." Sandra stares at me, trying her hardest to dim the light in her eyes, and not doing a very good job of it. "What do you say?"

I smile, take her in my arms. "I say yes, of course." Then I step back. "When will the girl arrive?" Sandra gives me another smile, this one almost shy. "That soon, huh?" I move past her, out the door. "I'll make sure the sheets are clean on the crib."

As it turns out, we don't need sheets, for from the moment the social worker places Fabianna into Sandra's arms, that's where she stays. The torments of withdrawal are hard enough to witness in adults. In an infant, it's heart-wrenching. The pain is intense, mostly from muscle cramps, but also from pounding headaches. An addict in withdrawal sweats, shivers, vomits and often loses control of their bowels and bladder. When their muscles cramp and knot, they double over or contort into agonizing shapes. To fight this, the body trembles, shakes, often violently. The addict cries out, screams, begging for something to ease the pain. Most often, they beg for the very drug that got them into this mess.

Fabianna also cries out, but she doesn't know for what, only that from the moment she emerged into the light of life, pain has been her world. She's lost in a cauldron of agony, her only lifeline the woman who holds her. Hours pass in screaming, tear-streaked anguish, then days, Sandra quietly reciting scriptures in Fabianna's ears, softly caressing her tiny hands, her arms, her feet, anything to let her know she's not alone. To witness this needless pain in one so young is nearly unendurable. The only thing worse would be to walk away from it.

Which is why we don't need the sheets, for to abandon Fabianna to the bed seems unthinkable. At night, she stays in our bedroom, in a small bassinet-like bed in between us, so we can be right next to her and soothe her through the night. During the day, when Sandra needs a break, I hold her. Or sometimes one of the kids. As a family, we are united—darkness may have accompanied this baby into the world, but it will not hold her. That's our job.

During the endless hours of that first night, Sandra tells me that Fabianna's father is married with three children, that Fabianna was born of a woman with whom the father was having an affair. Since the mother was a known addict, social services took custody of the baby in the hospital. The father was contacted but didn't want the child. After all, what would his wife and children think?

For days, all Fabianna can do is cry and shake. Even then, she's a beautiful child. Curly dark hair, bronze skin, eyes the color of ebony. She's half Mexican, half Puerto Rican, and wholly loved, not only by Sandra and myself but by all the kids—they come in, gather round, praying or giving encouragement to their littlest and newest sister. Jo-Jo is especially tender, and it pains me that he'll only know his new sister for a week or two before he leaves us.

At first, Fabianna sleeps only for moments at a time, those moments filled with spastic jerks, heartrending moans. But as the days pass, she slowly comes out of her withdrawal. She's so very tiny that when Sandra and I stand there—something we haven't done for years—the baby is almost lost in the immensity of our king-sized bed. I reach for my wife's hand, squeeze it gently. "She's perfect," I say. "Perfect."

And then, there's what I don't say. The name we're both thinking. Siloam. Because the agency has given us no indication of what the plan is. To me, it seems obvious—the mother is an addict, the father doesn't seem interested. Then, after a couple of weeks, we're informed that Fabianna's father has moved out—or been thrown out—of his family's home. Either way, I pray for him. But I also pray for Fabianna, that she becomes a part of a loving family, a Christ-centered family. A part of our family. Such a big name for such a small being; it would be a blessing to watch her grow into it.

On Fabianna's thirtieth day with us, my prayers are

answered, though hardly in the way I'd wished. My wife calls me at work to tell me that Fabianna's father has decided to take the baby.

"But..." My thoughts seem to blaze into flames, all I can think is that this is a mistake. A terrible mistake. "They told us the father didn't want her. I mean... he just moved out of his house, right? How's he going to care for her? She's so... so little and fragile."

I can hear the pain and effort in my wife's voice, repeating the words as calmly and clearly as she can. "The father has decided to take the baby. The decision has already been made. The case worker said to have Fabianna and all her belongings ready in two hours."

I feel my hand tightening around the phone, but all I say is, "I'm leaving work now, I'll be home soon."

And that's it. An hour and a half after I arrive home, Sandra walks Fabianna out to the waiting car, hands her over, tears streaming down her cheeks. We don't talk about it, because there's nothing to say. Our baby is gone; we will never see her again.

Later, we strip the tiny sheets from the mini bassinet, and after washing and drying them, we put them away in a closet, with the bassinet. It's a sad task, but one that needs to be done. Do not lose sight of the faithful One, I tell myself. Perhaps Fabianna will become her father's way back to the Lord—would I really want to stand in the way of that? Perhaps God is reminding us that while He always has a plan and a purpose, the plan isn't necessarily ours, and the purpose is not always to our liking.

Still, it's difficult. I find Sandra in the family room, hugging Jo-Jo. In just a few days, the boy will be returned to his mother. After drug addiction, after jail, after a lifetime of bad decisions, she has changed the course of her life. A glittering success story, a story for which I can only rejoice. Still, my heart aches. This is doubly true for Sandra.

When the day comes, we arrange with Johnson's mom to meet her at a local gas station. It's unusual for the foster parents to have face to face meetings with the biological parent, even more unusual for the foster parents to actually be the ones giving the child back. But that's the way we all want it.

Sandra is weeping even before we get there. It's all extremely emotional. We hug the mom, we hug Johnson, we tell them both how much we love them. We pray over them, asking God's blessing on them. My wife weeps the entire time. Tears of sadness, yes—but also tears of gratitude, for as difficult as this is, what a joy God has given us, this privilege of sowing His seeds. Others will reap the rewards, just as Sandra and I reap the rewards of Silas, Stephen, Seth, and Selah.

The van is silent as we return home. I glance into the rearview mirror, counting kids. One, two, three, four. Then I laugh at myself—what had I expected to see? No matter how much it hurts, we walk in obedience to what God calls us to do. Faith, I remind myself, is being sure of what we hope for and certain of what we do not see.

Chapter Eight

Simon and Sammie

October, 2011

It's been two weeks since Johnson left. Life is beginning to return to normal, the children and Sandra and I enjoying a quiet afternoon in the family room watching an old John Wayne western. Jimmy Stewart is in the middle of a long speech to his old friend John, when the siren goes off.

For a moment, all I do is stare at it, as if that should be enough of an answer. The siren ignores me and continues its wailing. If I were alone, I might cover the thing with a pillow, muffle the noise. I'm simply not ready for another challenge.

Apparently, Sandra is. She runs to the phone, her eyes glowing with excitement. My wife does this so much better than I—a week to mourn after a foster kid leaves, then back to serving God, ready and willing to love the next hurting child.

As she talks, the kids and I dart glances at her. I know what they're thinking—can we really go through this again? One more time, one more goodbye, can our hearts take any more?

"That's interesting," I hear Sandra say. "Can they go back? Ok, then—let me talk to my husband and get back to you." The person on the other end continues on, my wife nodding her head. "I understand, I do. We'll call back as soon as we can."

I stare at the TV screen, doggedly ignoring the fact that I'm the only one still watching. "There's a foster family in our church," Sandra tells us, her quiet voice overriding the gun battle on the screen. "They have a situation where their foster kids need to be removed. Two brothers, Jarred and Joseph. The case worker thought that since we attend the same church and live in the same area, the same school for the kids, our family would be a good match. A temporary placement," she adds, catching my eye, "until a permanent home can be found."

"We can talk about it this evening," I say. Then I reach for the TV control, turning up the volume. My way of ending the conversation.

The movie ends and flows into another—but I'm not really watching. The brothers live in our area—ok, fine. The foster parents go to our church—fine again. I can't stop thinking about Jo-Jo and Fabianna, about how they would have made the perfect additions to our forever family. Ok, they're gone, I understand that. But what about my wife's prayers? What about Siloam? She wants a little girl, a newborn, and I have this feeling—like an overwhelming need—that we will, at last, conceive, that Sandra will give birth to a precious little girl. *That's* our fifth child, I tell myself. *That's* what I want.

Because otherwise, it's just too hard. Four kids have come to us since Selah arrived. Four kids have gone away. Mindy and Audrey and Fabianna tore my heart open, Johnson yanked it out. I have nothing left to give. If the Lord won't bless us with a natural child, a child that can't be taken away, then I'm done. I quit. Let someone else take the brothers.

That's how I think of them—the brothers. Easier that way, more distance. The older brother is seven, the little one not quite a year and a half. They've already made the rounds to a number of foster homes, with two interrupted adoptions. And we'd only be a temporary home. It's a situation fraught with emotional landmines. Do I really want to invite that into my home?

And besides, in my heart, I know God is going to give us girls. I know it! I do my best to convince myself that if we take these boys in, even on a temporary basis, we might miss out on God's true plan for us. But it's a lie, and not even a very good one. Is God's arm really that short?

I pray during the movie, I pray all that afternoon and evening, I pray with my wife before bed. Sandra, great heart that she has, will always say yes. This time, perhaps I need to step up, protect her. Protect our children. Protect myself.

I was hungry and you gave me something to eat. I was thirsty and you gave me something to drink. I was a stranger and you invited me in. I needed clothes and you clothed me. I was sick and you looked after me. I was in prison and you came to visit me. (Matthew 25:35).

Try as I might to ignore these words, they play in

my mind, over and over again. Foster children are hungry for something more filling than food, thirsty for something more quenching than water. They are strangers even to their own families, with nowhere to turn. They are clothed in need and want, they are sick with sorrow and hurt, they are imprisoned by the trauma of their abuse.

By my fear of them. My fear of what it will cost. I remember a line from a Psalm—*You are the strength of my heart, and my portion forever.*

My portion. Forever. Is there anything I can't do through Him who gives me strength?

"Ok," I say to Sandra before turning off the light. "We'll take them. Jarred, and Joseph. But if it's temporary, let's make it quick. We can't wait for the foster agency to find them a family, we need to find one ourselves." I take her hand, making sure her eyes are looking into mine. "You understand? Another family."

Sandra just smiles.

The next day, the boys arrive. Jarred, at seven and a half and six years older than his little brother, is not happy about his new home. Not happy at all. This is his fifth foster care placement, Joseph's third. Two of the families had wanted to adopt the boys, had gotten far enough along in the process as to schedule an adoption date. For different reasons, both adoptions fell through. Like most foster children, the older brother was confused and blamed himself. Thankfully, the younger one had no idea what was going on. It doesn't matter what explanation is offered, foster kids can feel it in their bones—they're not good enough. But Jarred is way beyond that. He's disgusted. Adults have done nothing but disappoint him. I can see it in his eyes—all he expects is more of the same.

We show him the room he'll share with the boys, the dresser he can use for his clothes. He grimaces, then shrugs. "Who cares? Probably have to move tomorrow anyway."

I try not to react. Because, in truth, he's right. If we find a willing family, he'll be moving. We show him the rest of the house, but he pays little attention. His face is hard, his body tense. He's a handsome kid, or will be if he ever learns to smile—green eyes, a universe of freckles spread over his face, obviously smart, but introverted, wary, unwilling to let anything out.

His brother, Joseph, is a redheaded, blue-eyed toddler, smiling as little as his older brother. The case worker has told me that Jarred was removed from his home at three and a half. Joseph was taken into foster care upon birth, placed with his brother, the only constant in his life, which is the reason the agency is so determined to keep them together.

The very next day, Sandra and I begin asking people in our church about adopting the boys. Sandra approaches the task with a passion, for it breaks her heart to know how close Jarred and Joseph have twice come to being granted a forever home. There's only so much grief a child can bear, and these two have reached their limit—this time, Sandra will do whatever has to be done to ensure a successful adoption. Mountains will be moved, waters will be parted, and the boys *will be* adopted.

Only no one comes forward. Over the years, we've met and talked with many people who, because of our example, are open to adopting. Some tell us they have room for Joseph. Some say that Jarred will fit nicely. But no one is willing to take both.

Meanwhile, our children simply love having Jarred and Joseph in the house, and while this warm welcome makes it easier for the newcomers, we're also worried about them getting too close, forming bonds that will only mean more heartache for everyone when they leave. In a situation like this, it's difficult to know what the right course is.

After three days of asking and finding no takers, Sandra gets a look on her face that I know all too well. Very calm, very sure of herself. It's her we-need-to-talk look—but as she knows what it's about and I don't, my bet is that I won't be doing much of the talking. Sure enough, after she puts the kids to bed, we find ourselves face to face across the kitchen table.

One of the things I love best about my wife is that she just comes out and says what's on her mind, no beating around the bush, no attempt to hide the way she feels. Come to think of it, that's also the trait I find most annoying. "I want you to pray about adopting the boys."

Her request confuses me. "I, ah... I am praying, honey. Pretty much around the clock. No one's stepped up. Yet," I add quickly.

"What I mean is, pray about us adopting them."

"Us?" A hundred thoughts rush through my mind. Well, ok, a hundred variants of the same thought. No! These boys are *not* for us! Are they deserving of a forever home? Of course they are. And I'll help them find it. Only not here. "Sure, I'll pray about it," I say, mostly because that's what I'm required to say. What man of God refuses to ask his Master for advice? "But we have to remember, we've also been praying for another girl in the house. Two boys would be our limit with foster care. We take them in, it might mean we're losing out on more girls. I just... I don't know if the boys are right for us."

Sandra takes my hand. "Thirty days. Pray with me for thirty days. In thirty days, if a family appears, then we'll know."

"Thirty days," I agree. But my heart is clouded.

I don't go so far as to mark the calendar, but in my mind, the days are clearly numbered. "Find a family?" I ask every day when I arrive home from work.

And Sandra answers, "No. But there's always tomorrow."

It becomes almost a joke, a routine. Find a family today? No, but there's always tomorrow.

Except that we're running out of tomorrows.

The 29th day of our prayer vigil falls on a Saturday. This particular Saturday, the entire church gathers for our twice-yearly service outreach day. It's an amazing time, people going here and there to provide service to those in need. We clean, we paint, a few of us even do a little building. The best part is that the children get to join us, experience the joy of giving to others, and to see that joy mirrored in the faces of those receiving.

Before going out, we gather at the church for a time of worship. The members of my family don't usually all get to sit together, it's actually kind of impressive— Sandra and I and six children, with my father sitting at the end. We take up almost an entire row! Then the band begins to play, we rise and sing and release ourselves into the glorious music. I sink into my worship, lose myself in the words, the melody, the joining of so many voices all rising to heaven.

After a few minutes, I turn my head, check on the kids. All I mean to do is make sure no one needs help, but what I see sends shivers up and down my spine—Jarred, eyes closed, hands lifted high, singing his heart out. The kid's face is almost glowing, this boy who's been through so much, and had so much taken from him. Now, here he is, lost in worship. Or, maybe more correctly, found in worship.

Staring at him, I feel the presence of the Lord hovering over me. I hear His voice. A single word. *Simon.*

Simon? All the children in our family have been renamed with biblical names beginning with an "S"—but the name Simon isn't one I've ever considered. I take out my phone and do a quick search. The meaning of Simon is 'the one who hears God'.

The one who hears God. I gaze at Jarred, arms upraised, eyes closed, words of praise on his lips. He's at peace. And suddenly, so am I, for God is telling me that this young boy—a boy who's been through more trials than many adults face in a lifetime and is still able to stand and sing praise—this boy is being given a new name. Simon.

I look further down the row and see my dad holding Joseph. At that very moment, Joseph turns, staring at me, and I hear the Voice again. This time, the word is Samuel. I again check my phone. Samuel means 'the God who hears'.

I begin to shake, my knees wobbling, my heart racing. Simon, the one who hears God, and Samuel, the God who hears.

But God isn't done with me, for He knows only too well my doubting heart. And doubt—despite the miracle of the names—is what I'm left with. My thinking goes something like this—Surely God wants us to have a balanced family. And five boys, one girl isn't balanced. It isn't fair to Selah who wants a sister. It isn't fair to my wife who wants another daughter. And with six kids, we won't be able to foster any longer. No more chances. Ok, their names will be Simon and Samuel. I'll be sure to tell their new parents.

Then the celebration ends, the entire church exiting for our day of service to the community, and I have little time to think about it. And little desire.

The next day, Sunday is the 30th day of our prayer commitment. Not just any Sunday, either—it's Orphan Sunday at our church, the one Sunday a year we devote to children without families. It's also one of the few times that I'm actually able to take part in the adult service, for as Children's Pastor, I'm almost always with the kids. But here I am, the 30th day of prayer, Orphans Sunday, front and center before the entire congregation. And still undecided about Jarred and Joseph.

God has some great sense of humor, that's for sure.

I sit through two amazing services, God continuing to rock me to the core. *Simon*—I hear the name like someone whispering in my ear. *Samuel*. I should be totally convicted, but I can't help thinking maybe I'm getting it wrong. Every time I make a decision, the word pops into my mind. *But.* It sputters on like an old broken engine. But, but, but, but, but. God has spoken, it's me that continues in my unbelief. I know my fear, my lack of faith. But...

After the second service, as confused as ever, I rise and walk into the foyer where my wife is managing an information booth, talking to people about how they can foster or adopt. I step to the side, waiting for a moment when she isn't busy.

The moment never arrives. Instead, the light of the sun is blotted out, a man, the size of Goliath, is moving to my side. I've never seen a man that tall. Not up close. Lots of muscles, too. And totally bald! I attempt to say hello, but whatever leaks out of my mouth sounds more like Eap, eap, eap.

"My name's John," he says to me. He catches my eye—to do this, John must look almost straight down. "I have a word for you and your wife."

I'm thinking, *a word for us? I don't even know this guy!* But then I realize that saying no to a guy who could probably crush cement blocks back into sand might not be the wisest approach.

"A word? Sure. Thanks." And that's as much as I can get out.

"If you and your wife would hold hands?" Sandra joins me, gripping my hand, facing John. We watch John settle into himself, his face relaxing, a slight smile on his lips. "You're about to make a big decision," he tells us. "But you're confused." His smile grows larger. "Don't be. The Lord is leading you just where He wants you to go. Take the step He's asking you to take, a step of faith. Say yes. Trust Him."

Yesterday, I was given the names of the boys. Today, we're given a prophecy. Whatever lingering doubt I harbor melts away, I feel peace wash over me and through me. Jarred and Joseph—Simon and Samuel—I have been given two new sons. And they have been given a home. A forever home. If I waffle now, it's no longer doubt—it's defiance.

A few days later, Sandra and I sit Jarred down and ask him if he wants to be a part of our family. If he wants to be our son. I glance over at Sandra. Her face is radiant, her smile dazzling.

Then I look at Jarred. His eyes are aimed in our direction, but it's the vacant, thousand-yard stare I've seen in returning war veterans. "Sure," he says. "Yeah." The words could have been uttered with more emotion by the Mr. Potato Head in our toy chest.

I open my mouth, thinking to reassure the boy, tell him that this time, it will happen. But he's heard that before, too. He's heard it all. And this is what he's learned—adults lie.

Another idea pops into my mind, and without thinking about it, I say, "Jarred, when we adopt you, you can have a new name. In church the other day, God whispered to me that maybe you'd like the name Simon." This is new, so Jarred looks up, interested. "Simon means the one who hears God. It's a really special name, and I hope you like it because you're a really special boy."

"Simon." Jarred's mouth rolls around the word like it's some form of exotic new candy. As he does this, his entire face slowly lights up, like someone turning up the wattage of a lamp. "I do like it! Simon!"

Sandra and I laugh and hug the boy. "Ok, Simon," I say, "go tell your brothers and sister about your new name."

And that's it. Our green-eyed boy is now Simon. His brother is now Samuel, though we all call him Sammie. The names instantly take, no one ever makes a slip. Simon and Sammie. God hears and is heard. What more could I ask for?

Unfortunately, Simon—despite his new name—quickly falls back into doubt and distrust, especially as the day of adoption draws nearer. We let him listen in when we call the foster care agency, telling the case worker how delighted we'd be to include Jarred and Joseph as part of our family, to give them a forever home. It does no good. Every day, he goes to his dresser drawers, opening them, closing them—I can almost see him calculating how long it will take to pack the stuff into a suitcase.

As the days go by, the tension in his small face grows. I would do anything to relieve him of it, but there's nothing to be done other than hurry along the adoption process. The one thing that helps are my sons, Stephen, Seth, and Silas. Simon has become good friends with them all—their presence, their common histories accomplish more than any words.

And then the day arrives. January 26, 2012. To my mind, there's nothing quite like going to court, sitting in that solemn place, the judge in his high seat, almost like a king staring down on his court. It's not a giddy moment. In fact, for Simon and Sammie, it's downright terrifying. Especially for Simon, who would run out if he could. Better than once again hearing that it won't happen, that he won't be adopted, that something went wrong. And knowing in his heart that he's the something.

The judge listens to this lawyer, that lawyer, the guardian ad litem, a few others. Then the truly remarkable moment when the gavel bangs down, hard enough to send the kids jumping, the judge declaring that now and forever more, Sandra and I are the new parents of Simon James Hogue and Samuel James Hogue."

Adoption Day Simon & Sammie.

For a moment, Simon just stares at the judge, his mouth wide with wonder. The judge laughs and says, "Son, it's finished. This is your new family. You'll never have to move again."

"You hear that?" Sandra says, kneeling down in front of Simon. "You'll never, ever have to move!"

A smile grows on Simon's face, grows like a new sun rising above what had been an endless night, towering shafts of light radiating outward, brightening everything they touch. It might be the most beautiful smile I've ever seen.

And then we go home. It's a different home than the one we left this morning. A brighter home, a happier home. A forever home.

Your Honor Sammie Hogue.

Simon and Sammie.

Chapter Nine

Endings and Beginnings

Parenthood of any type is a constant struggle. For Sandra and I, and for the children as well, there is an extra component, a hardship, and a blessing rolled into one—we are not a biological entity. Truly, God puts the lonely into families. Each of our children can say, "I was chosen! I'm *that* special!" And then deal with the feelings arising from another set of parents who didn't want them or who couldn't care for them.

In the same way, Sandra and I can know that God chose us. Most Christians realize that having faith can be a difficult task—but how do we respond to the faith He shows in us? Out of all the parents in the world, we were chosen! Ten times chosen!

Then someone comes along in a supermarket, or a clothing store, and says, "Wow. You've got a regular baseball team there. Any of them yours?"

My first impulse is to... well, let's just say I overcome my first impulse. I understand what they mean—adoption, especially adoption of more than one or two kids, is not the American norm. I use the opportunity to show them my heart, to explain the need. Usually, they listen politely, the men clapping me on the shoulder and wishing me well, the women smiling brightly. But I can almost read the thought bubbles floating above their heads—*These people are nuts!*

Sometimes they ask if we're Mormons. Or Catholics. Or maybe we just don't have a TV. Whatever is said, Sandra and I try to handle it with humor and acceptance and to teach the kids to do the same. Still, it can be wearing.

The most difficult response to handle is sadness. Certain people, when we tell them what we're doing, what we believe, look at us like instead of gathering to ourselves the most precious of gifts, we've thrown it all away. Instead of seeing joy and love and peace, they see only a horrible burden. Some of them even say it—"What about vacations? Or a night out? You don't actually take them along, do you? I mean, how do you, how do you..."

"Afford the finer things in life?" I finish for them.

"Well... yeah."

"Children *are* the finer things in life."

I try to explain, but all I see in their faces is sadness and pity. I may never have the fancy vacations, high-end sports cars, or expensive, tailored suits sure to impress the congregations I visit. For far too many people, the American Dream has been perverted into a never-ending pleasure-fest, and children only get in the way. Hard enough to have a good life with children of your own, why take on other people's burdens? These folks have willingly put on blinders, they're unable to see the needs of those Jesus most loves, unwilling to hear their cries, unwilling to step forward and be part of the solution.

Carrying on a conversation with these people has always been a trial for me. Yet as time goes on, I'm more and more drawn to it. Because every once in a while, one of these scoffer's dull eyes grow bright. "Really?" they say. "You've adopted them, all of them? How does that work? I mean, you seem so..." I wait, letting the person come to it by themselves. "So, I don't know... so fulfilled."

Fulfilled. Not happy, not relaxed, certainly not the easy-come, easy-go otter I'd once thought myself to be. But yes... fulfilled. I wish I had time to tell of all the great examples I've had over the years, all the wonderful advice and help I've received from people who know more and have done more. Instead, I start at the beginning—which is also the end. For there's only one name I need mention. Jesus.

As I've said, it doesn't happen often. People are generally willing to support the idea of rescuing orphans, but they'd rather do it from afar, by providing funds or food or clothing. Which is all well and good, and necessary. Still, they are missing out on the bigger prize, the delight of giving a home to a homeless child, of becoming a parent to the parentless, of filling a heart with love where before there was only darkness.

And therein lies my problem. I've now worked as the children's pastor at Calvary Christian for over ten years, and the daily grind has begun to lose its glimmer. Don't get me wrong, it's still a great job. Calvary is still a wonderful, thriving church. And Jim Raley, the head pastor, is still as dynamic and far-seeing as he was in 2001 when I was hired. And yet... I'm starting to feel hemmed in, a sensation akin to seeing kids in the van who haven't yet arrived. But whereas more children in the van would be a blessing both to them and to the children we already have, thinking that my job is no longer enough seems a betrayal of those who have put their trust in me.

As a remedy, I work harder, pray longer, plead more fervently with my Maker to rid me of dissatisfaction. None of it does any good. The only time I'm free of doubt are those moments when I'm talking with potential adoptive parents, especially when I see the light dawn in their eyes, the realization that by saving a single child, just one, the entire world is changed forever!

The one course of action I don't take is to confide in Sandra. In many ways, my wife has had a harder life than I have. Her childhood had its own challenges, and her marriage to me has presented a few issues as well. Through it all, she has persevered. More than persevered—she has thrived, taken what life has offered and spun it into spiritual gold. Calvary is her home, a place of acceptance and refuge, a family that knows her and loves her and always welcomes her presence. How could I ever ask her to leave?

And so I bounce between questions that can't be answered. Confusion becomes my morning wake up call, reliable as an alarm clock, and frustration the clothes I wear throughout the day. It's simply not tolerable, and this is exactly what I tell God as I pray. Intolerable, Lord. Intolerable. I need an answer.

Prepare. This is the single word that comes back to me.

Prepare for what? I ask. But that's all I get.

Prepare.

Oddly enough, my mind goes back to a time before we'd joined Calvary, when I was the Youth Pastor at New Covenant. It was a small church, and after five years, in 2001, I decided to leave, to take the position I now have. I made an appointment with the head pastor, and after telling him of my decision, he closed his eyes and began to speak a word over me. He had given me my first opportunity, and so I listened, but it was a very odd word he spoke, and I can't say that I understood it.

"Stephen, New Covenant has been your first ministry step. Calvary will be your second. Your third step will be a national ministry, but take care, for you will need Calvary to get you to that third step."

I nodded and put a look on my face like I understood what he was saying. But really, it was like buying a house, and while at the realtor's office signing the papers, before you've actually moved in, the realtor says, "Hey, wait till you see the next house I'm going to sell you!" I hadn't even started at Calvary, and my pastor's telling me that the ministry after will be a national ministry. This disturbed me, even more so in that he told our congregation about his word, and people would approach me, congratulate me. I didn't know how to respond.

Then we left, moved to Ormond Beach, and I forgot all about it. Until now, that is. *Prepare.* God does not speak without purpose, so I take the word, put it on like a new pair of glasses, studying my life.

Sandra and I have always been careful with money, but in the months that follow, we save even more, putting any extra funds into a special bank account. Sandra knows something is up, though I do my best to keep my thoughts hidden. It's really not that difficult, because I have nothing to actually think about. Prepare for what? If she asked me, I couldn't say. All I really know is that I'm being presented with a bucket-load of questions, and not a single answer. Am I willing to walk away from the paycheck I receive at Calvary? How will I support my family? And walk away to where? And what about the stability so necessary to my children?

A year goes by, and in that time, it becomes almost impossible to be wholly present for my job. I feel like a fake, like all I'm doing is going through the motions. At staff meetings, I'm about as active as a bear in winter. What is my vision for the Kids ministry? I no longer have one. Everything in my future is enveloped in fog. I perform my daily tasks, but something is missing. Something vital. And I hate it, hate knowing that I could do a better job, be a better person.

Prepare.

To say the least, it's a difficult time. A number of months after Simon and Sammie are adopted, I decide that I've had it with not knowing God's will for me and my family. I need some answers. Fasting and praying has worked in the past, and that's what I do now.

It takes four days. I'm in my daughter's bathroom, cleaning like a madman, when the divine download finally comes, stopping me cold, taking away my breath. I see a crystal-clear vision of my wife and I standing on a stage in front of a large church congregation, sharing our story, the story of God's heart for His orphans. People are crying. And I can almost hear God speaking to me. *Go. This is the message you are to share. You have done much. Now do more.*

More? Before this very moment, I wouldn't have thought that possible. We've adopted six children and fostered many others, I was running a ministry with over 350 kids in it. How much more could I possibly do? Of course, this is a worldly way of thinking about it—I can only do so much, I'm only one man, my wife and I only one couple.

But in an instant, all my doubts are swept away, thick tangles of storm clouds parting to reveal a brilliant sun. I understand the vision, not as the world would have me understand, for all the questions that existed a moment before still exist. Now, however, those questions are transformed by the light of God's purpose, a purpose that can only be walked by faith. I have no idea of how to accomplish the task being asked of me—nor do I need to figure it out. No matter where God calls us, no matter how difficult His request, His Word is true and just, the path he lays out for us is the very best place to be.

I hurry from Selah's bathroom, eager to share the good news with my wife. Fulltime Orphans Ministry! Sandra is delighted. None of the questions that have been plaguing me come up. Where I've had to pray and fast, Sandra knows right away—God will provide.

It only hits me later that morning, as I pull into my parking spot at Calvary Christian—moving on means stepping down. A simple thought, an obvious thought, yet the avalanche of feelings it triggers in my heart threatens to bury me. I get out of my car, walk into the building, passing people I've been working with for years. My friends, my family. I want to hug each one of them, pat them on the back, cry on their shoulders. Another part of me screams, *Get it together, Stephen!*

Ok, it's a big move I'm thinking of making, leaving behind everyone I've known and everything I've done. With no security net. I need some time to settle into it. Only reasonable. I'll wait a week, tell people then.

The next week comes and goes, then another and another. Then a month. Two months. Three. Every two weeks, I look at the paycheck I've just received, and I think, *Are you crazy? A great job, a great church, a great paycheck? You want to throw that away, live on a missionary's budget? With six kids?*

That's what I say to myself. Because it's easier than the truth—and the truth is, I'm scared. Each time I think of scheduling the meeting with my head pastor, my heart starts beating so loud that I have to hurry away for fear he'll mistake it for a knocking on the door and invite me in.

The months pass, the kids grow. Stephen especially is shooting upwards. He asks to help me with the children's ministry, and I let him, thinking little of it. He wants to please me, it's only natural. But it's more than that, and in the moments when I step back and watch him, the love he has for ministering to the younger ones is clearly evident. I remember a few years back. He set up kids church in our playroom, equipped with a puppet stage and sound system. He really blew me away by writing his own kids' church lessons.

One day, he comes up to me and asks, "Dad—how old do I have to be to do your job?"

I smile at him. "Why, you think I need some help?"

He gives me a reproving frown. "I don't mean *your* job, Dad. I mean, how old do I have to be to become a children's pastor?"

So we talk about it. Stephen is both earnest and committed—he wants to be a children's pastor. A kid who started like Stephen did, with so much to hold against the world, now wants to work with God in shepherding those most vulnerable. Amazing, absolutely amazing!

And God isn't even half done. A few weeks later, Seth visits me in my study. "Hey, Dad," he says. "I know what my first car is going to be."

"Really? Your first car?" I put down the paper I'm working on and turn to him. "Ok, what is it?"

Grinning, he says, "An RV!"

"Because you like camping so much?"

"No, Dad." I'm treated to a scolding shake of his head, as though I'm a student who's not been paying proper attention. "Because God's called me to be a children's evangelist. I'm going to travel all around the country telling kids about Jesus! It's going to be great!"

The words of Jesus come to me, *You have hidden these things from the wise and learned, and revealed them to little children.* These two children, who were given such a difficult road to travel, are ready to march out, forgetting the past, reaching for the prize. And here I am, the same prize awaiting me, hanging on for dear life.

The very next day, I make an appointment to see the head pastor. And yes, I'm nervous. I can't help but think that my resignation will strike him as a betrayal. Am I absolutely sure I'm not doing this for my own benefit? Absolutely sure the vision I saw means what I believe it means?

Soul-searching—the use of brutal self-honesty to make sure one is not bending the will of God to serve oneself—is good, even righteous. Doubt, on the other hand, is not. Most often, doubt is little more than a questioning of His will. And doubt is what creeps into my thoughts.

But even when one doubts, God is merciful. Just before my appointment with the head pastor, I walk into my office, see that I have a voicemail. Hitting the play button, I hear a sweet voice identifying herself and saying that she's heard about our desire to start an Orphan's Ministry and would our family like to visit her church and be a part of the Orphan Care event they're planning.

Just then, Sandra walks into the room. Without a word, I play the message for her. She looks me in the eyes and says, "There's confirmation." Then, hand in hand, we walk to our meeting with the head pastor and his wife.

After exchanging greetings and small talk, I ignore the doubts crowding my mind and simply say it. "Pastor, Sandra, and I feel that God is calling us to share God's heart for the orphan and fatherless to His people. There are kids who are hurting, kids who need homes, kids who need parents. In Florida, twenty thousand plus kids in out-of-home care, and in our local area, 1200. Most of all, they need to see God working in their lives. We would have to step down to do this." I briefly tell him of the past two years, how I've searched my heart, what God has shown me.

When I stop, for a moment, all I can hear is the blood pounding in my ears. What will he say? Dumb idea? Get real, Stephen? What?

"Stephen..." Just this one word lifts my eyes and my heart, for it radiates love. "Stephen... this is right for you and Sandra. This is your heart. God is going to use you in an amazing way in this new season."

And that quickly, the heavy load I've been carrying for the past two years floats away. The four of us all cry, then talk, then cry some more. I tell them that we don't want to leave the church or the city. This is our home. Instead, I want to be based out of Calvary, I want to develop and lead the Orphan Care Ministry from here.

"Yes," he says. The word is so simple, so sweet. "That would be good. Too much change can be confusing. We can set you up with an office in the building."

In my wildest dreams, I couldn't have imagined such a wonderful meeting. But not in God's dreams. We all hug, the love in the air almost thick enough to cut.

God must truly enjoy watching His children, the same as I enjoy watching mine. How He must laugh when Sandra and I discover that the very first church we will be speaking at is none other than New Covenant, where it all started for me. I can almost hear my old pastor's voice. *Your third step will be a national ministry, but take care, for you will need Calvary to get you to that third step.*

And now, here we are. My heart's knocking as I walk to the podium, but there's no doubt in me, none at all. How could there be? If God is for us, who can be against us? I look out at the congregation and smile, knowing that the next time I speak here, there will be children in the audience that are not here today, children that have not yet been introduced to their forever parents, to their forever home. Perhaps those children will call Sandra 'mother', call me 'father.' More likely, their parents sit in the audience, not yet aware of what a blessing God is about to drop into their laps.

Chapter Ten

Siloam

December, 2012

Over the years, we have sent our family profile off to various adoption agencies. With every paint job, every bedroom remodel, Sandra d iligently updates the profiles, so that any moms-to-be can see how we live and where we live.

She also regularly updates the profiles we've given to numerous adoption agencies. Every time our profile is shown to an expectant mother, Sandra and I are notified. Over the years, we've learned not to get excited, for the same thing happens, over and over again—the mom-to-be takes one look at the many children we already have and goes on to the next profile. With all the time and work it takes to create and update these family profiles, we've never received even one call. Not even one.

So, when we get a call just before Christmas from Highlands Maternity Home in Hot Springs, Arkansas, asking us if they can show our profile to a young expectant mother, we say yes, then go back to life as usual, thinking nothing more about it.

A few weeks later, in January, I'm sitting in my church office, working on way too many projects at once, papers strewn here, there and everywhere, when I get a call from Jay Mooney, director of Hillcrest Children's Home in Arkansas, where Highlands Maternity is located. The first thing he says is, "She liked your profile."

I'm not quite sure how to respond. I mean, Sandra put a lot of time into it, did an incredible job of documenting life in the Hogue residence. So I simply say, "Good, good," trying to keep my voice neutral.

"No, Stephen, what I mean is, she's chosen you and Sandra as parents for her child."

I stutter out something not quite intelligible— apparently, Jay is used to this type of response, for all he does is laugh. Then he tells me a rather long and convoluted story. I don't interrupt him, not even once. It might be the most entrancing tale I've ever heard.

"The mom-to-be was eighteen when she got pregnant. A sad story, and unfortunately, all too common. The girl was running hard, living a wild life, fun at any cost. You know the drill. She liked to party, and she wasn't all that concerned with who or how many or when the party might end. Then she found herself pregnant. No idea of who the father might be."

"Now, this is where it gets interesting. A youth pastor recommends she come here, to Highlands Maternity. For a girl with her lifestyle, it's surprising she'd pay any attention at all to what a youth pastor might say, and even more surprising that she'd actually take his advice. But glory to God, she does. She's been with us for five months now."

"At our home, life is life, the mother, the unborn child, one's not less important than the other. So while the mother's with us, we do more than tend to her physical health, we do our best to tend to those hurts inside that have never healed. Most of the young women who come here have had a rough life. As I believe you know from reading your profile, there's only one true answer, and our staff tries to reflect that by showing love and understanding, where these girls are accustomed to condemnation. This young lady, though, this one..." Jay laughs again, a full-throated roar. "God did a work on her, I'll tell you that! Put her face to face with the life she'd chosen, the decisions she'd made. Oh, yes, God dealt with her. He spoke to her. He healed her and restored her. It was a wonder to watch, a true miracle!"

"And she's appreciative. So appreciative that she surrenders her life to Christ. Now that's not the end of the story, just the beginning. After a whole lot of prayer, she feels the call to be a minister of the gospel. How's that for you? Arrives on our doorstep all broken and alone, winds up saved and wanting to go to Bible College! And after a whole lot more prayer, she decides that if she's going to fulfill this calling, if she's going truly begin her life anew, she needs to place her baby up for adoption."

"With all my heart, I believe this young woman has never made a more difficult decision. Nor a braver one. Because, you know, I hear it all the time, and so do they... the birth mom getting accused of abandoning her baby. Even from well-meaning Christians. We rush to judgment, we assume the mom is selfish, cold-hearted, that she just doesn't want to take responsibility. Stephen, my friend, if that were true, she would've chosen the easy way out and signed up for an abortion. No, indeed—these women are heroes. They carry life within for nine months, go through all the ups and downs of pregnancy, physically give birth, hold their child... and then let go. And they let go for the best of reasons so that the child might have a better life. It's an act of selflessness. An act of love. Pure love."

"Long story short..." I hear Jay chuckling. "Well, maybe not so short. My apologies. Anyway, before taking on the task of looking through family profiles— we pretty much have a library of them—her case manager has her figure out the type of family she'd like for her baby. The young lady comes up with three preferences. First, the parents need to be in full-time ministry. Second, they have to be under forty years of age. And third, she wants the wife to be a stay-at-home mom. Well, that narrowed it down considerably, and, tell you the truth, the case manager thought your family would be a good fit. Problem was, the mom-to-be looks at the six kids you already have and goes right to the next profile."

"Now, the weeks are going by, our young lady isn't getting any less pregnant. Only she just can't decide. So the case manager gives her your profile again, asks her to take another look. And I have to say, that's some profile you put together. Pictures of all your children, nice family room, music room—really like the pics of the kids playing instruments, by the way—the church where you work, kids you work with. Pretty much your whole life. But it isn't till she gets to the pictures of your

124

girl Selah's room that she decides. She sees the crib in the corner, with butterflies and flowers, in purple and pink—those are her favorite colors, purple and pink. And the matching crib skirt, the mobile, the stuffed toys... she tells the case manager, these are the folks, they're ready. And here I am, telling you. By the way, the baby is a girl. You ok with that?"

"Ok? Am I ok?" My voice is shaking, I notice I've risen out of my chair. I force myself back down. "No, Mr. Mooney, I don't think ok is the word for it. Not even close. Overjoyed, maybe. Humbled to my core. Overwhelmed. Grateful, though that seems too small a word for what I feel." Then, "I have to tell my wife. I mean, right now, I have to, I..." I find myself on my feet again, though I don't remember getting up. "Thanks for your call, Jay. We'll call you later."

The good news is that I don't get a ticket rushing home. Come to think of it, good news is the only news I have. Normally, I get home around five. It's now one-thirty. Normally, I walk in. Today, I'm running. Or maybe I'm skipping, it's hard to tell. And my face—well, I can't see my face, but I'm quite sure there's nothing normal about it.

As soon as Sandra sees me, she knows something's up. "What are you doing home so early? she asks."

"I got a call today."

My wife's eyes widen, she takes a step closer.

"From the adoption place in Arkansas."

Sandra now looks as though she might explode. "They chose us!" I say. She runs to me, leaps in my arms, squealing with delight. "We're going to have our baby girl! Our Siloam!"

When she could at last speak, she asked, "When's the mom due?"

"Early March."

Sandra calls Jay Mooney in Arkansas, making sure we have everything in order. But we don't announce it. We don't even tell our kids. It's a secret, a wonderful secret, and we wait for the perfect time to make it known. Sandra wants to tell our extended family in person.

Two weeks later, we host a gathering at our home. Sandra's sisters and mother are there, my sister and her family, my dad, his new wife. We're all just hanging out, eating, talking, laughing, having a great time. Which is when Sandra says, "Hey, everyone—Stephen and I were sent this promotional video from a maternity home in Arkansas. I'm going to put it on, we can all watch."

The idea of watching an adoption promo is greeted with reserved acceptance. The family already knows that Sandra and I are a little weird, a little off-center. My dad tries to leave, but I corral him back. "It's actually a pretty good promo," I tell him.

The video comes on, we see our very own birth mom-to-be, standing proud. Well, actually, sitting proud. In the video, she's six months pregnant. And she starts to talk, sharing her testimony, most of which Jay Mooney has told me. She tells how much the baby means to her, the life she carries, and how very important it is to her that this baby finds a home, and find Christ in that home.

Far to the side, I've picked up my video camera, doing my best to surreptitiously capture their faces. As the video ends, Sandra stands in front of the TV, her smile bright as the noonday sun. "The reason I asked you to watch this is... the girl in the video has chosen Stephen and I to adopt her baby! She's due March sixth!"

The already quiet room descends for a few moments into absolute silence—not only don't they talk, it seems they've all forgotten how to breathe. Then the place erupts, laughing and crying and shouts of joy. I'm crying, too, even as I continue videoing the scene. To have so much support, so much love... it's overwhelming. Everyone's asking when the baby will come, what they can do to help. Totally overwhelming.

Then the day passes, everyone leaves, and it's back to the hourly struggles and triumphs of raising six kids. Soon to be seven. I can't rid myself of the thought. Seven. Perhaps it's no coincidence that we've had to wait seven years for her.

As January bleeds into February, the anticipation is almost too much to bear. My wife is a master planner, care of our children scheduled to the minute, their needs organized and compartmentalized. Lately, she's been nesting—cleaning and organizing and putting items in bins, making room in closets and dressers. But there's no way to know exactly when the baby will come. Babies are born when they're born, sometimes on the due date, often not. We just have to be ready. Our plan is to fly to Arkansas the moment we hear she's gone into labor. The birth mom is allowing Sandra to be in the delivery room, to actually be the one who cuts the umbilical cord! Sandra is beyond ecstatic!

I'm booked to appear at a children's ministry

conference in California from the seventeenth through the twenty-first of February. It's an important conference, one that I scheduled long ago. I pray that the delivery date will be on time—the sixth of March. But as the date draws nearer, Sandra receives a call from the Arkansas social worker—the birth mom had to see her doctor twice this week because of abdominal pain. Which means that the birth could come early.

February 16th comes, the day I'm to fly to San Diego. The due date is still March 6th, but with a very large question mark. It's a long flight, I arrive exhausted, fall into my hotel bed. The next morning, I call Sandra, she tells me there's nothing new to report. I eat a quick breakfast, then do my best to concentrate on the conference schedule—but I can't. My mind is filled with thoughts about my new baby girl... our baby. Siloam.

Late on the last day of the conference, at nine that evening, Sandra calls. Her voice is panicked. "They're taking her to the hospital! She may give birth tonight!"

I want to race out the door, but after calling the airport, I realize there's nowhere to go—the earliest plane won't leave until tomorrow morning. Sandra encounters the same situation. Other than calling back and forth, trying to reassure each other, there's nothing we can do.

As early as possible the next morning, Sandra and I make our separate ways to our separate airports, board our separate planes. The best I've managed is a two-layover flight. At the first layover, I call Sandra, who tells me our mom has started labor. At the second layover, I discover the baby has been born. Sandra is disappointed that she couldn't be there for the birth, cut the cord—but it's a small disappointment compared to the joy of knowing the baby and mother are healthy.

Sandra has arrived before me and rented a car, we take off for the hospital about three seconds after my plane has landed. The baby's now a couple of hours old and doing fine. We have an hour drive to the hospital. I try to talk about the conference in CA, but we keep returning to the subject of Siloam- whether we will hold her right away or wait for birth mom to offer, what we're going to say to birth mom, how we will tame our joy in the midst of her sorrow, ... and on and on. We've never met any of our children's birth moms, so we're newbies at this. We try not to speed.

At the hospital, much as we want to rush right in, we are told by the social worker that the birth mom has requested twenty-four hours with the baby before letting go. This sends an electric shock down my throat, pulsing into my heart. It's only natural, I tell myself— she's just given birth, she wants to hold her baby, even for just a day.

"Arkansas is very sensitive to the needs of the birth mother," the social worker goes on. Something in her voice focuses my attention. Something sharp, almost cutting. I feel Sandra's hand clutching mine. "Please understand—no matter what she says today, or tomorrow, or even next week, the birth mother has ten days to change her mind." The woman makes sure our eyes are on her. "Do you understand?" The woman waits until we nod. "Even after the baby is given to you, even when you're the ones caring for her and feeding her and changing her, you'll need to stay in Garland County. Once the ten-day mark has passed, you'll appear before a judge, where you will be given the right to go back to Florida. Now...", a sudden, eager smile appears on her face, "let's go see how mom and baby are doing."

We walk into a hospital room similar in detail to hundred-thousand other. And yet wholly unique, for there in the bed is our mother, tenderly holding the baby. Holding Siloam. She quickly glances at us with a timid smile and returns her gaze back to the baby. Sandra walks to one side of the bed, I to the other, trying not to focus all of our attention on the baby. It's hard. We've waited seven years for this moment.

"It's nice to meet you in person," Sandra says simply, a hand reaching out to touch the mom's shoulder. Then, eyes brimming, lowering her eyes to the baby, "She's beautiful."

We spend just a few minutes talking with the birth mom, cooing at Siloam—then we leave, giving her the time alone that she's requested. It's been an incredibly long few days for us, we go to our temporary apartment at the maternity home, rest up for the next day, making sure we have everything Siloam will need.

But the next day, when we go back to the hospital, everything has changed. The case worker meets us at the entrance, ushers us away from the room being used for the mom and baby.

"She wants more time," the woman tells us. "She's struggling. Letting a baby go is always difficult."

"Maybe if we talk to her..." Sandra begins, but the case worker shakes her head.

"Not a good idea. And anyway, it isn't allowed."

I reach for Sandra's hand, find it shaking. We are

ushered into a lobby area just outside the maternity ward, find a couple of chairs away from the family and friends waiting to visit other babies. I do the only thing I know to do—pray. *Lord, I know you haven't brought us this far just to leave us. You are here, with us, with Siloam, with her mother. Your love surrounds us, supports us. What is there to fear? Whatever we want, whatever we believe should happen, it is You in control. You will not let us fall, You will guide us and comfort us. We want Your will to be done. Tell us what to do, Lord, and we will do it.*

After that, we post a vague social media announcement, asking our friends to pray for birth mom and for us and for God's perfect will. Sandra texts those closest to us about the possibility of us coming home without our baby and gives them the real situation, asking for prayer for all involved.

The case worker comes back in a couple of hours. I glance at the wall clock—it seems like days have passed. Her pleasant face is scrunched with excitement. "Mom's ready to give you the baby and would like you to join her family in a prayer of dedication."

"Her family?" I say.

"The girl's father is with her. Sweet man. He didn't tell her to do anything, no pressure at all—just encouraged her to follow God's plan."

Hand in hand, accompanied by the case worker, we walk to the mom's room, entering quietly. Her eyes are red and puffy, the glimmering tracks of her tears still evident. The baby is held tightly to her chest, rigid, as though any movement would expose a hole in her heart. Her father, the baby's grandfather, stands next to her, a rugged, worn man, 100% Filipino. He nods, smiling slightly, introduces himself. He shares with us that he and his wife are in agreement with the adoption plan. Relief fills the room and disarms any feelings of animosity.

The hospital is required to follow a very specific procedure—the nurse is to cut off the birth mom's plastic bracelet, put a new bracelet on the adoptive mom. Witnesses must be present. But as the nurse steps forward, the birth mom's dad announces that his daughter would like to pray for the baby, and then he would like to pray over Sandra and me as the new parents. We are momentarily overwhelmed. Humbled. This girl, so young, yet so willing to follow God. And her father, there to support his daughter, to welcome her back despite what others might call the shame she's brought him.

The mom holds Siloam close, praying blessings, and protection, a broken, ragged prayer, selfless and courageous. She asks God to always fill her baby's heart with her love, even though they are far apart, and that in growing up, that her child always walks in accordance with God's will, that she always know and trust in God's plan. Tears decorate her words, falling on the baby, a baptism of love. Sandra and I are weeping at the sight of such sacrificial love.

Then her father prays - over his daughter, his granddaughter, and over us. It's a beautiful prayer, full of hope and dedication and prophetic declaration. When he's done, a nurse cuts the bracelet off the birth mom's wrist, lifting the baby up and placing her on a cart. The cart is wheeled to the nurse's station. A second nurse places a new bracelet around Sandra's wrist, the official sign that she is now the mother.

In silence, the birth mom gathers her personal belongings and is helped into a wheelchair. One of the nurses wheels her, accompanied by her father, out the door and down the hallway; out of our sight. As she disappears, I feel both elated and sorrowful. This young girl has laid down her life for another, then given that life to us to raise.

"I can't believe this is happening," Sandra says, her voice trembling. "Two mommas in love with the same baby girl, and I get to keep her." She glances down the hall again, smiling. "How courageous."

We go back to our apartment in the guest quarters of Highland Maternity, Sandra holding our tiny bundle as tightly to her chest as had the birth mom. Because we both know—it's not over. We still have ten days to wait, ten nerve-racking days. The stress of this falls mainly on Sandra, for we haven't forgotten that six other children need us, need our love and assurance. So the next day, I fly back to our home in Florida, arriving that evening bone-weary. Sandra looks forward to the skin on skin bonding and healthy attachment she will get to enjoy without the distractions of her normal routine and homeschooling six children. She assures me that she will make video calls daily to continue "homeschooling" the children at home, so I don't have to. School was never my thing. And so homeschooling our kids was definitely the primary role for Sandra. I was the principal and took care of all disciplinary action, which she very much appreciated.

I arrive home. I'm a little disappointed in my

reception, which is no reception at all. I set my bags down, call out. Nothing. *Ungrateful little...*

They seem to hit me all at once, bursting out of closets, around corners, all six piling into me, wrestling me to the ground, laughing at their good joke. I lay there laughing with them, pulling them closer.

Six children, soon to be seven. What could be better? *Eight.*

I sit up, Silas and Sammie tumbling off my chest. "Who said that?" But all I see are giggling, laughing children.

Eight. God has a very good sense of humor, as I'm soon to find out.

Courtday Siloam.

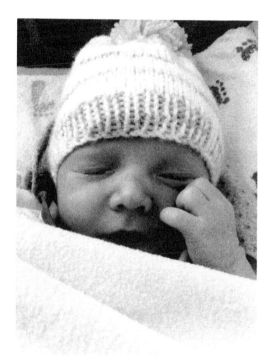

Newborn Siloam.

Chapter Eleven

Sarai

March, 2013

The next day is full of surprises. Upon awakening, I discover that Sandra has started a contest with all our Facebook friends, the challenge being to guess the name of our newest child. Even before I've sat down to my first cup of coffee, the appellations start pouring in, everything from Sarah to Seraphim. The oddest guess is Samson, and while it's true that I'm an admirer of strong women, the poor fellow who's suggested the name is disappointed when I tell him that long hair or short, Samson will not be winning any gold medals. Not in this contest.

I also get a reminder from Sandra about a judicial court review she wants me to attend. Judicial reviews are held every six months for children in foster care, their stated purpose to ensure that the child's case plan is being rigorously followed, or to allow for changes should they be needed. In this instance, the review is for three children taken in by their grandparents after the mother's drug and alcohol abuse grew too severe.

A few months before, the grandmother, Tamara, had asked Sandra for help. Tamara had explained that she and her husband simply couldn't handle three small children. They lived in a condo, both worked full-time jobs and raising a year-old girl and two boys, ages four and five, took more energy than they had. She wanted to know if Sandra could put her into contact with a Christian couple willing to adopt all three kids and still allow the grandparents to be involved.

Three children that young are a lot to take on all at once. Some good friends of ours were interested in the two boys, but not the girl. When the boys began to spend occasional nights at our friends' house, in order to give the grandparents a night off, Sandra and I would take the girl. It really wasn't much trouble, our kids loved little Bailee and treated her like a princess, feeding her and clothing her and caring for her. In fact, the visits worked out so well that the court listed us as a non-relative care placement. We didn't think much about this—it's a legal term that allowed the grandparents to leave Bailee with us and at the same time provided both parties indemnity in case of mishaps.

And now back to God's very good sense of humor. I show up to the hearing wearing my usual attire, which is to say no one would ever mistake me for one of the lawyers. I greet Tamara, give a few tickles to Bailee, who frowns and gives me what can only be called a growl. At sixteen months old, the grandparents are Bailee's fourth home. I'd be growling, too. She's been in court more often than many seasoned criminals.

The judge comes in. We all rise. For a moment, I wonder where the two boys are—but then I completely

Sarai.

forget about them as the judge begins speaking because the review isn't about the boys, who've already been placed with our friends. It's about Bailee.

"Are Sandra and Stephen Hogue present?" the judge asks.

I fumble up from my seat, suddenly sorry that I *don't* look like a lawyer. "Ah, I'm Stephen Hogue, your honor. My wife's, ah... tending to one of our children."

"Ok, then, Mr. Hogue. The Guardian Ad Litem and the lawyers involved have already reviewed the request for non-relative placement, and as the current relatives charged with care also agree, you are now awarded guardianship of the child. Court papers will be sent to all parties concerned." And before I can say a word, he bangs down his gavel, rises, and leaves through a rear door.

Tamara has Bailee in her arms. She stands, handing the girl to me. The look on my face must fall a little short of love, joy, and peace, for Tamara says, "You have done this before, haven't you, Steve?"

"Sure, sure." I smile at Bailee, she frowns back at me. "I'm just, just... I thought you wanted all three kids together?"

Tamara's smile widens, she claps her hands. "Yes! That's exactly what I've been praying. For months and months. Then I realized—God *is* placing them together, just not in the way I'd imagined. Your good friends are taking the boys, you'll have Bailee—so of course, they'll see each other. And both families have no problem with including me and Denny in their plans." She grips my arm. "Bless you, Steve. Bless Sandra." She turns to leave, and quick as that, she's gone.

I shrug, gazing at my newest child. "Guess it's just you and me, kid." Bailee reaches out, trying to punch me in the nose.

Back at my car, I strap Bailee into her seat and call Sandra, who is still in Arkansas with Siloam. I want to surprise her, but instead, simply blurt out my own amazement. "They gave us Bailee."

For a moment, all I hear is a sweet burbling, the cooing of our youngest but now only second newest child. "What are you talking about?" Sandra finally manages. Do you mean, they gave us Bailee?"

"What it means is, she's sitting in the back seat, all strapped in, and I'm taking her home. The judge gave us temporary guardianship. She will stay with us until a permanent placement is found.

Once back at the house, the kids and I have a party. In the space of 48 hours, Selah now has two sisters. Hopefully has two sisters. There's still so much that can happen. Selah doesn't share my worries. "Finally," she says, her voice triumphant. She lifts Bailee off the ground, dancing around the room. "Finally!"

What I love about children is that they have so much more faith than adults. Or perhaps it's just a simpler faith, void of all the complexities we grownups throw into our own paths. Either way, while I'm worrying that Siloam's birth mom might change her mind, the kids are pestering me about not being left behind this time. They want to go to Arkansas.

"You can't be serious," my sister tells me. "Seven kids in a van for that long? And one of them you hardly even know? That's crazy!"

"Some people would say the crazy part is having all these kids in the first place." It's a thought that makes me smile. Beam, actually. Eight children in a little over eight years. Yeah, most definitely—crazy. Of course, more than a few people said that of Jesus. And Paul. And Peter. So crazy or not, I'm in good company. "Anyway," I add, "Bailee can't come. We're only her guardians, we'd need a court order to take her out of state. No time for that."

My sister shakes her head. "Crazy."

At 9:20 on the morning of the tenth day, when the birth mom doesn't change her mind, it becomes official. Siloam is ours. The kids and I all celebrate, then plan the trip. I ask Tamara to take Bailee back for a few nights, knowing that it takes a judge's approval to leave the state with a child in state custody. And since Sandra's the planner, she helps me come up with the list: pack sandwiches, snacks, pjs, outfits for court, then wake up early the next morning and hustle out to the van. Except for brief stops, we drive through lunch, through dinner, past the sunset and deep into the night. It's two hours past midnight when we finally arrive. I'm exhausted. So is Sandra. But newborns rarely sleep through the night, and this is especially true of a newborn meeting her six siblings for the first time. All the kids want a turn holding their new sister, and good sport that she is, Sandra makes sure it's all recorded on her camera.

When the festivities are done, we all fall into an exhausted sleep, filling every bed, couch, chair, and corner. Then, all too early the next morning, we get up and ready ourselves for court. The judge comes in, sees an entire tribe of Hogues standing before her and smiles, obviously amused. Our kids all smile back — court pros, every one of them. Between the lot of us, we probably have more court experience than most of the lawyers present.

In relatively little time, the judge signs the order stating we can leave the state of Arkansas with our new baby, then wishes us well. Silence might be the court's rule, but we're as noisy as a flock of magpies as we file out the big doors and down the steps, heading towards our van. What an amazing two weeks! I get everyone strapped in while Sandra holds Siloam, then it's back the way we came. This time, there's no way we can make it in a single day. Siloam isn't at all happy about her car seat, she needs to be fed while the van isn't moving. We overnight at a motel, then continue on, tired but wholly contented.

* * *

After a short time home, after we've all caught our

breath and caught up on our sleep, we pick up Bailee from her grandmother's. As days pass, the family begins to see a different side of Bailee. We start calling her our 'spicy girl.' She isn't very happy, she cries at the smallest incident, and she will hit people without warning or provocation. Kids need stability and structure in their lives—this is true with any age child, and it's something little Bailee has missed out on. Her brothers remember living with their mother, but Bailee was moved into a family member's home almost from birth. Which might have been okay if she'd stayed there, but it was only the first of many homes.

Her acting out is exacerbated, as we discover, by a delay in her language skills. She has trouble expressing what she wants and is quickly frustrated when we don't understand her. Sandra and I are also frustrated, for Bailee rarely gives us enough time to decipher her requests before bursting into tears or striking out.

Adults can fall into the trap of thinking that the younger a child is, the easier it will be to retrain them. Sometimes this is true. Often, though, the lessons of our early months are ingrained at a more primitive level. Bailee has learned that her caretakers change often and therefore causing attachment and trust issues. Like many children in the foster care system, it takes consistent, firm parenting, with clear boundaries and unconditional love.

Children have few options, especially the younger ones. They can't change their environment, their verbal skills are minimal, and they're almost completely dependent on adults for the basics of life. If Bailee is to become the glorious person God intends, it's vitally important that the adults in her life provide a patient, consistent approach. Teaching a child to love and trust requires loving and trustworthy caretakers, ones who cannot be shaken. Even then, it takes time.

It also takes the entire family, and our family is a blessing indeed, for they have lived it. Children who've been abused or neglected or abandoned can go either way—they can become empathetic and understanding, or they can decide that the best way to avoid abuse is to become the abuser. Our children, though they slip at times, the same as we all slip, are wonderful examples of how light and love can triumph. Even more than Sandra and I, they are Bailee's best teachers.

And Bailee responds. Not quickly, certainly not all at once—but week by week, month by month, her behavior becomes more accepting, more able to take in the love we offer. It's a totally awesome experience to watch, this poor little child who was lost, now actually smiling when a brother or sister enters the room.

After several months, we receive some awkward news. Someone in Bailee's birth family wants to adopt her - the same family that took care of her for the first 6 months of her little life. The foster agency already knows we're willing to adopt—but being willing isn't the same as saying, "Wait a minute, this is Bailee's home, this is where she belongs." Without a fight, the court will almost certainly side with the member of the child's birth family. And who's to say that isn't right? Perhaps it would be better for Bailee to live with and know her aunts and uncles and cousins. Am I so wise that I can know for sure?

The answer to this dilemma comes from the most

unexpected of people. Bailee's grandmother, Tamara, on one of her visits to our house, tells us that she has no doubt about her granddaughter being exactly where she's supposed to be. Because she's playing with Bailee, a noisy game of coochie-coo, I'm not sure I've heard correctly.

"You don't think she'd be better off with a family member?"

Tamara sets Bailee down, turns to me. "I prayed for Bailee, then you and Sandra came to me. The other family didn't." And when I still look quizzical, "I've learned plenty in my life, Steve. One of those things is this—you don't argue with God. He answers prayer, well then, that's the answer. Bailee is where she belongs. Besides, the other family stepped in at the beginning, and then they gave her to me to take care of without any explanation. Just 'come get her. We can't keep her anymore.'

End of discussion. An hour later, I call the child welfare agency, let the case manager know that not only are we willing to adopt Bailee, but we're willing to contest any plan that moves her from our home. Instead of the lecture I'm expecting, the case manager calmly tells me what the process is—the adoption team will interview both parties and decide. That's it.

Two weeks later, on the day of our interview, Sandra and I enter a quiet room in the center of the agency building. I thought it would be a small meeting, but the chairs around the long table are all filled—case manager, Guardian Ad Litem, state attorney, adoption specialist, and a whole lot of others. We're asked to sit at the end, facing the group. I feel like a goldfish in a glass bowl. Except that goldfish don't sweat. Intimidating, to say the least, especially when the state attorney starts off by saying, "You're aware that someone in Bailee's birth family would like to adopt the child. Why do you think your family is a better fit?"

My mouth opens, but my mind has gone blank. No, that's not quite right—I have thoughts, it's just that they aren't very helpful. Such as, *What if we're not a better fit? The other couple has two kids, we have seven. And they're family. What if I'm wrong about this? What if I'm seeking my will and not His?*

Fortunately, it's Sandra who answers. Her voice is gentle, but it cannot mask her passion, her assurance. She speaks of our love, our experience, she talks about brothers and sisters who can help encourage and teach Bailee, about the structure we provide, the nurturing and the care. She ensures that Bailee will be in touch with her brothers, who now live with our friends and attend our church.

As she talks, as I watch the people watching her, their eyes full of concern, I feel a peace come into the room. It hits me that we already know most everyone seated at the table, some of them for years. Many of them have been in our home, seen the rooms, the photos decorating the walls, the attention we've given to even those children slated to stay only a short while. Another part of me chimes in—*Sure, but every other child they've offered has had no other option. We were the only family who wanted them. Now, there's a choice.*

When my turn to answer comes, I let go of all the bickering inside my head and simply speak my heart.

"Sandra and I want only what's best for Bailee." My voice is trembling, I do my best to pull it back in, to speak with a calmness I don't feel. "We know most of you. We trust you. If a decision is made that places Bailee in our home, our entire family will be delighted. She's already a daughter and a sister to us. But it's her good that we're here for, not our own. We're ok with that."

"It's a big family," one of the interviewers comments. "How will you give Bailee the one-on-one time she needs?"

Again, I just speak my heart. "It's a challenge, for sure. A huge challenge. Each of our children has a different schedule, different likes and dislikes, different needs. And my schedule is fairly hectic as well. Sandra and I have to go out of our way to physically touch each child, to spend alone-time with them. Sometimes that involves rolling around on the floor, wrestling. Or sitting quietly on the couch, watching a movie. Or coaching them with their homework. And there's always one or two kids who are having a hard week and need some extra help." I think about each of them, their faces, their smiles. And I realize I'm smiling, too. "Truthfully, I wouldn't have it any other way. The struggle to get to know them, to keep up with them—it's the best part of being a parent."

A woman clears her throat, asks the next question. We do our best to give an honest and complete answer. Then on to the next question. And the next, and the next.

At some point, the questions end, we rise, shake hands with everyone present and leave. Walking out,

I feel I've run a mental and emotional gauntlet, and I can see from the way Sandra leans on me as we trudge towards the car that she feels the same. The process has not left me optimistic. But as I review the answers we've given, I'm sure we did our best. The rest is up to God. On the way back, we pray that Bailee is guided to the right home; that whichever home is picked, she grows up to love God, serve God and live for Him all the days of her life.

And that's all there is to it. We wait for the other family to have their interview, we wait for a call. I suspect that Sandra and I are about as good at waiting as most people, which is to say, not very. But we put up a brave front. This is especially hard to pull off around Bailee, who, like most kids, has an intuitive sense that something is up. To compensate, we give her extra time with us, which only makes her more suspicious. Smart kid.

It's amazing how slowly a day can take to tick by. Multiply that by seven, and I'm almost out of my mind by the time the adoption specialist finally calls, informing Sandra that we are free to pursue adoption, that our family has the agency's full support. Sandra thanks her, tears streaming down her face, then thanks her a few more times. "They chose us!" she screams as she disconnects. Sandra grabs my hands, dancing me around the room. "They chose us, they chose us, they chose us!"

I take her in my arms and laugh. "Yeah, I sort of got that part already."

After we tell the kids, call relatives and friends, it occurs to me that Bailee will need a new name. For each of the other kids, the Spirit has whispered in my ear. But so far, nothing has come to me. And there's not much time to ponder it, because we need to file the adoption papers, and the new name has to be on them. It also concerns me that Tamara and Denny might have a problem with a name change. To them, their grandchild has always been Bailee.

Most people in this modern world don't realize the importance of a name. At one time, a child's name was considered prophetic. Abraham named his son Isaac, which means 'laughter.' Samuel means 'the God who hears.' Names are like guideposts—long after father and mother are gone, the guidepost will remain.

For our family, the standard has always been a name beginning with 'S' and coming from the Bible. Sandra and I always loved the name Sarai, which was Sarah's name before God changed it. The meaning of Sarai is 'my princess', and from the way Bailee has been passed around, she could use some of that. Her hitting and bad moods have diminished, but she needs constant attention and affirmation. She's always wanting to be held, to be noticed. The problem is, if one of us isn't noticing her, the child will go off with anyone holding out a hand to her. Fine if the hand belongs to Seth or Stephen or Silas, but we worry whenever we're in a crowded place.

Oddly enough, Sandra has already begun to call Bailee 'my little princess.' Sandra has an intuitive sense about these things, and right now, Bailee desperately needs to learn attachment—not simply a princess, but *my* princess. As we pray about it, ponder over it, Sandra and I more and more come to believe that Sarai is the name God wishes. It's a royal name, but also a grounding name, a name that places the girl in relation to others.

Seeing God in action always amazes me, and that's exactly what happens once we announce the new name. Bailee is never heard again, Sarai is here to stay. No mistakes, no blunders, no 'oops, sorry'—every kid is perfect, as though Sarai had never had another name. More amazing still, Sarai herself seems comfortable with the change. As I said, God in action.

Tamara and Denny are also supportive. Or, as Tamara tells us, Sandra and I are her parents now, we have every right to do what we believe is best. "It might take some getting used to," she says—and then with a wink—"But I think Denny and I are still young enough to learn a thing or two."

At last, a few months later, the day comes, that magical day we've all been waiting for—adoption day! There's really nothing like it. Even though we've done it before, it's always sparkling new, a true miracle. We've invited friends and family, there are balloons, cameras, and no one is without a smile. This includes the judge. Dependency judges oversee some horribly sad cases. Often, their decisions are not between good and bad, but between bad and worse. They love happy outcomes as much as anyone, and perhaps more than most.

The crowd quiets as the bailiff walks in, and silences completely when he says, "All rise." Then the judge enters, the bailiff announcing him, and we all sit. Sandra and I, with Sarai, are front and center. Standing nearby are the people necessary for the adoption to go forward—case manager, attorneys, adoption specialist.

One of the attorneys begins a formal reading of the case, ending with a question to Sandra—"Do you still wish to adopt this child, and if so, why?

This is the point in the proceedings where my wife starts to cry. Happens every time. She shares her heart with the lawyer, with the judge, with the world, a bunched tissue in either hand. And here's a secret—if I were to turn around, no doubt I'd spot more than a few sniffling faces. They are tears of joy, tears of faith.

Once the attorney finishes, it's the judge's turn. We all know what he's about to say, and it doesn't diminish the impact in the least. "And now, Sandra and Stephen Hogue, this child will be yours as if naturally born to you." Music to our ears.

Adoption Day Sarai.

What a wonderful statement! What a beautiful moment! Behind us, people begin to cheer and take pictures. Everyone crowds around, congratulating us, congratulating little Sarai. We pose to take pictures with the judge. I don't know if the sun has suddenly come out from behind a cloud, or if the Lord of our hearts is making His pleasure known, but the vast room seems to have suddenly brightened. And why not? If there's a better feeling than giving a child a new life, a new destiny, Jesus honored, and God exalted, I've yet to find it.

Adoption Day Sarai.

Happy Adoption Day Sarai!

Chapter Twelve

A Place at the Table

Let me tell you a story. Most of you know it but listen anyway. Because beneath what you know, this is a story that encompasses the heart of orphan care.

For many years, David served King Saul, both in battle, killing Goliath and winning battles, and at Saul's home, where David eased the king's headaches by playing his harp. Despite this, Saul grew to hate and fear the younger man and repeatedly tried to kill David. Jonathan, though he was Saul's son, was David's good friend, and did his best to intervene, but all he could accomplish was to delay the final battle between his father and David. In that battle, both Saul and Jonathan were slain.

When the nurse caring for Jonathan's son, Mephibosheth, heard that both Jonathan and Saul had died, she became terrified. She fled, taking the young Mephibosheth with her. But there was an accident, the nurse tripped, and the boy was thrown down, suffering an injury that left him crippled. On that day, Mephibosheth lost his father, his grandfather, his legs, and his position as the royal heir. He was robbed of his future and left without hope.

This story is an incredible picture of what far too many kids in foster care face today. They have been thrown down by the very ones who were supposed to lift them up. They have suffered harm at the hands of those entrusted with their care. They have been separated from their parents, their homes, their hope. The very name, Mephibosheth, means 'great shame.' This is how our modern-day orphans, our foster children, view themselves—not worthy of family, not fit for a forever home. With all their belongings packed into used suitcases, or lacking that plastic trash bags, they are carted from one place to another. They view love as a gift meant for real sons, real daughters. Before they have truly begun life, they have lost their place in the world.

Mephibosheth went to live in a town called Lo Debar, which means 'a place without pasture, without promise.' He had no way to generate income, nothing he could offer anyone. It was a fate worse than poverty—Mephibosheth had become valueless, one more piece of trash to be discarded into the pit of Lo Debar. Unless King David discovered where he'd been carted off to and came to kill his enemy's grandson, this would be Mephibosheth's life, living at the whim of those stronger and more able.

But something happened to Mephibosheth that completely changed his circumstances. He was correct in his fear of King David, for the custom back then was for the new king to kill anyone even remotely related to the old king, thus ensuring no one from the old family would rise up in challenge. David did the opposite—he asked his court, "Who from the house of Saul is left so I may show kindness to him?"

I imagine David's question was greeted by dumb silence. What type of king showed kindness to his adversary? What type of king cared for others before himself? What type of king stopped the proceedings of his court to ask if one of his enemies could be found so that he might help them? For a long, long moment, I suspect David's advisors remained unmoving and quiet. Finally, a man named Ziba stepped forward. "A son of Jonathan still lives," he told the king. "He is crippled in both feet, a pauper in the town of Lo Debar." David immediately requested that the son be brought to him.

Ziba had Mephibosheth transported from Lo Debar then carried in to see David. The young man must have been terrified. As terrified as I remember Seth when he was being pulled from the caseworker's car, carried in screaming and crying. Set down before David, Mephibosheth bowed his trembling head to the ground and said, "What is your servant, that you should notice a dead dog like me?"

A dead dog. I've never heard those exact words come from a foster child's mouth, but close enough. Worthless. Ugly. Stupid. Dumb. Loser. That's what Mephibosheth felt, that's who he'd become. But not to David. David saw the grandson of Saul, the man God had anointed to lead Israel. He saw the son of a brave man and true friend. He saw a chance to share with Mephibosheth some of the mercy and grace God had shown to him. Instead of harming the young man, David ordered that all the lands once owned by

Jonathan and by Saul be restored to Mephibosheth. He also appointed Ziba and his sons to work the land for Mephibosheth.

At this point, David had been merciful in a manner few have ever equaled. But then he went further. Much further. From that day on, he announced, Mephibosheth was to eat at the king's table, an equal to the king's own sons. The people listening must have struggled to keep their mouths from dropping open. A king inviting the crippled grandson of his former enemy to eat at his table, a place reserved for royalty? Why would he do that? Did Mephibosheth have some hidden wealth or power? Did he perhaps hold the understanding of questions for which David sought answers?

No. Mephibosheth was exactly as he appeared. He was crippled, he was helpless. Both his heart and his body were broken.

The name David means 'beloved.' He had an intimate relationship with the Lord. The 'Beloved' often reflected on the many gifts God had bestowed on him and the tender mercies he'd been granted. He forgave because he had been forgiven. He showed mercy because God was merciful with him. He loved others because God had first loved him. And he rejoiced to be able to give Mephibosheth a place at the table.

Some foster parents take in children because they feel it their duty. Perhaps it is—but it's also their privilege, a wondrous opportunity to give back a small portion of what God has given us. We, too, love because of Him who loved us first. We are merciful because mercy has been shown to us. We help others because God lends us the strength, the vision, and the passion of His Son.

What foster child doesn't feel the way Mephibosheth felt? A cripple. A dead dog. An orphan with no future other than the barren land of Lo Debar. As a people who have been showered with the love of God, who value the sacrifice of his Son, it is our calling to transfer this love to the lost and dying.

When Mephibosheth came to David, he was a mess. Were we any less of a mess when we first laid our burdens before God? Our own sin had thrown us down, crippled us. But merciful God, in His unfailing love, in His great compassion, has blotted out our sin and given us a place at His table. Mephibosheth had nothing of value to offer David, and on the surface, neither do the kids in the foster care system have anything to offer us. But then, isn't that the way we all must appear to God? Thank God He sees us as we could be, not as we are.

Every day, over 400,000 children are listed as dependents of the state, living in foster care. Over 20,000 teens age out of foster homes each year, never having found a forever family. That's almost 50 kids a day. Yet despite the ones who age out, the ones who are returned to parents, the ones who are adopted, the number of children living foster care only goes up. Why? Because new cases of abuse and neglect are also rising.

There is an answer, but it doesn't come from the government. Government agencies, though full of well-meaning people, are concerned with life's essentials—food, clothing, shelter. If the problem could be so simply remedied, it would have disappeared long ago. Harder by far to supply what's truly needed—love, compassion, understanding, patience, healing. Harder,

I say, but hardly impossible. David showed us the way. All we need do is step out in faith, one hand grasping the hand of a foster child, the other latched securely in His.

Chapter Thirteen

Solomon and Sophia

December, 2015

Another Christmas coming up, thank you, Lord!

What's not to love about Christmas? The birth of Light, heaven opening to us, the singing, the praise, the presents. Even with eight kids... no, make that *especially* with eight kids, it's a glorious time of the year. Except...

Except I find myself in a store, the wrong number of items in my shopping cart. The same thing happened yesterday. And the day before that. Maybe I'm pushing too hard, working too much. I stare down, count again. Ten toothbrushes.

But why ten? Three times in a row.

I go home, deftly hiding my newest stocking stuffers, then settle down for some personal time with Samuel, who's five.

"Daddy," he says, curling up next to me on the couch, "I know what I want for my birthday."

"Your birthday? That isn't for a while. Why don't you think about what you want for Christmas?"

He gives me a playful shove. "Cause you already got our presents, that's why." He giggles, and I know without asking—he's found my stash of goodies hidden in the garage. "And anyway, this is a bigger present."

"Bigger?"

His eyes grow serious. "Way bigger."

I stare at him for a moment, wondering what it could be. A train set? A real train? "Ok, I give up. What do you want for your birthday?"

"A brother. One I can play with."

"Sammie... aren't the others letting you play with them?"

He shakes his head, frustrated with how slow adults can be. "I mean, a brother my age. A *new* brother."

I try to ponder how to handle this. "You think I can just go to the store and get you a brother?"

Sammie's face twists upwards, searching the ceiling for an answer. Then he flashes me a smile filled with trust and hope and adoration. "Ok," he says.

A short while later, I have the same conversation with Selah. She would like a sister, one her age. The only real difference in their requests is that Selah is old enough to realize that I can't pop down to the local 'Brothers & Sisters 'R Us' and pick up the latest model. At least, I think she's old enough.

After talking about it, Sandra and I begin an internet search for a brother and sister in foster care, ages five and ten. The thing is—and this even though I am weekly telling audiences about the number of needy foster kids—the odds of finding a brother and sister of those ages, both children already freed for adoption... well, let's just say, if someone told me this was their approach, I wouldn't be overly optimistic.

The problem with low expectations is that they are all too often made into a reality, and sure enough, in the days that follow, though we comb through database after database, we find no matches. Also, there's collateral damage—by reviewing so many stories, by witnessing the faces of so many orphans, our hearts are repeatedly torn open. And since it's Sandra doing most of the searching, it's Sandra doing most of the suffering. Thousands of kids are in need, we have room for only two. Time after time, Sandra comes to me, holding photos, printouts, tears wetting her cheeks. I want to tell her that saving them all is beyond our capabilities—but isn't that *exactly* what I'm asking of God? I want to save every one of them. There's not a kid that Sandra tells me about that doesn't deserve a happy ending. Or more to the point of our mission, a happy beginning.

But all I say is, "They'll come to us. In His timing and in His way, they'll come." I believe this, but at the same time, it seems a woefully inadequate response.

For the past six years, Sandra has volunteered at a local church, where she assists foster families shopping in the church's Orphan Care Resource Closet. The church loves her, for not only is Sandra a whiz with stretching a budget, but her warm, inclusive nature puts those coming in to shop at ease. After all, Sandra is one of them. She talks their language, the difficulties, and joys of fostering, the fears, the stress, the incredible thrill of seeing a child blossom and overcome.

This week, because of her orphan search, she's a little off. Most of the parents don't notice, for Sandra puts on her service face, cheerful and supportive. But one lady, a foster mom of a ten-year-old girl and someone Sandra has gotten to know, waits for a quiet moment and asks her what's going on. With a heavy heart, Sandra shares her desire to adopt a brother and sister, five and ten. "But we haven't found them. I know they're out there, I'm sure of it!"

The woman places a hand on Sandra's arm. "Christmas... it's a time of miracles, don't you think? You know my ten-year-old is free for adoption, right?" Sandra nods, the woman smiles. "But I never told you she has a five-year-old brother. Different foster homes, so your search probably missed them." The woman goes through her purse, coming up with a card. On it are written the name and number of her foster girl's case worker. "Merry Christmas."

Their names are Laura and Kenneth. It's a Friday night, but Sandra calls the case worker's number anyway, leaving a message. We've been looking all over the state, and our answer is practically in our own backyard! I don't know if God has heard our pleas or the pleas of these two kids—either way, it's a glorious turn of events!

To top it off, the case worker, Mrs. Moore, calls back that very night—which would have been wonderful but for the news she gives us. Another couple is interested in the kids, and though they haven't been matched yet, their paperwork is in and moving in the right direction. We understand what she means—most people wishing to adopt would prefer a baby or a toddler, so when older siblings are freed for adoption and someone shows interest, the agency jumps on it. Even so, we request to meet with the adoption team. The least that can happen is that they'll know we are interested, keep us in mind for other kids.

Because Christmas is fast approaching, we don't expect anything to happen until after the new year. In January, we call the agency, letting them know we're still interested in the two children or other siblings who may be available in the same age range. A few weeks later, the adoption specialist calls and sets up a date when we can meet.

When the date arrives, Sandra and I drive down to the social services building, walk into a small room with a round table, all of the seats filled. And again, I find myself somewhat intimidated, the questions coming at us non-stop.

"You've adopted eight children, Mr. and Mrs. Hogue—why do you want to adopt two more?"

"Can you provide for ten children?"

"Are you capable of handling special needs kids?"

"Do you believe in therapy?"

"Do you believe in medication if necessary?"

"How will you help Laura and Kenneth acclimate to their new home?"

"Are your children open to adding another brother and sister?"

As before, the answers we give are heartfelt and simple. We leave the meeting, and once back in the car, pray that God guides the outcome in accordance with His will.

And then we wait. It seems like an eternity, but a team of people deciding the path of a child's life is never going to be a speedy process. It takes a month before the adoption specialist, Mrs. Thomas, calls us, leaving an upbeat but altogether vague message. The message is clarified when Sandra calls back—the team has found our family to be a positive match for the two children. When Mrs. Thomas tells us that the first couple has no children, we're completely dumbfounded. Why choose us?

"Simple, really," Mrs. Thomas says. "You've adopted six other children from the agency. We know you can handle the behavior, the physical and emotional challenges. They both have speech impediments. Laura's is rather severe."

Kenneth and Laura live about five miles from each other, approximately forty-five minutes from us. Our first visit is scheduled for mid-February. At this point, we don't tell our children what we're doing, for they hardly need more disappointment in their lives should the visit not go smoothly. And, to tell the truth, though we feel called to take them in, give them a forever home, Sandra and I are somewhat overwhelmed by their special needs. Also... ten kids? The thought rattles around in my brain, looking for a place to settle.

Our first meeting is at Laura's home. Kenneth's foster parents drive him over, so we can visit both children at the same time. When initially meeting kids, many adults feel the need to pull the children into their world—this usually entails sitting around and asking them loads of questions. Bad idea. Because the adult already holds all the advantages. If you want to build a relationship, enter the child's world, do what the child does. Play. And that's what we do. Tag, volleyball, pushing them on swings.

Laura is especially adept at the card game Uno. In fact, she beats both Sandra and myself. She's friendly and active and understands why we're visiting, that we might become her new foster parents. The girl has olive skin, high, prominent cheekbones, dark brown eyes, and short, dark curly hair. Both she and her brother seem well-adjusted and happy, but Laura's speech is almost unintelligible. On several occasions, we ask her to repeat her words, and a few times resort to having her foster parents interpret for us.

Her brother, Kenneth, is similar in appearance, but with long, thick eyelashes and a scattering of freckles. He seems more reserved, perhaps because he's younger and doesn't understand the purpose of our meeting. His speech is marred by a slight lisp, but nothing that hinders understanding. Of more concern are his legs—they appear weak, giving the boy an awkward walk. Despite this, he seems to be active and healthy.

Solomon.

Sophia.

All in all, we enjoy our visit with the kids. For children raised by mentally ill, substance-abusing parents, children who'd suffered neglect and severe physical abuse, their spirits are amazingly resilient. Truly, God has given these little ones, in their simple faith, abilities that we who have learned so much more can only marvel at. Sandra and I thank the foster parents for letting us visit and ask when we can come again.

After a number of visits, we ask for and receive permission to have Kenneth and Laura stay at our home over spring break. Going from eight to ten kids is a big step, we want to see how the new mix will work before committing, and especially before revealing the plan to our children. For now, all we say is that two foster children will stay with us while their parents are out of town, which is true, but not wholly true.

Honestly, having two kids in our home not acclimated to our rules, structure, and routine is more of a challenge than I'd imagined. During the week, Kenneth has accidents in his pants while playing outside and while sleeping at night. He seems in a daze, unsure of why he's here or what he's supposed to do. Laura is quicker to adjust, but her severe speech impairment is a problem. Our children understand some of her words, but it's necessary to ask her to repeat things over and over. To her credit, Laura reacts to this good-naturedly, as patient with them as they are with her.

It's also a lot of work, ten kids at home for nine days, no school. On a small budget, it takes a good deal of creative parenting. We travel to local parks, to the beach, to a variety of free or low-cost exhibits, we play in our yard, and Laura beats everyone at Uno.

And then it's over. Once the dust has settled, and our tribe is back to normal—well, as normal as our family is ever likely to become—we convene a family meeting. Before getting into what I need to say, I ask the kids how they enjoyed having Laura and Kenneth at our home. Their answers don't surprise me, for over the last week and a half, I've watched them interact. Sure enough, one by one, the kids all respond positively. At that point, Sandra and I explain about the option of Laura and Kenneth coming to live with us permanently.

"What do you think?" Sandra asks.

For a moment, no one speaks. Then another and another, the silence growing stronger. Finally, Seth says, "So... you're saying we get to keep them?"

"Maybe," I say, then launch into the complicated process involved in adoption.

Halfway through my explanation, Stephen nudges

Seth, winking at him. "Yeah, we get to keep them," he says, loud enough for everyone to hear.

More visits are scheduled. Samuel is giddy about having Kenneth as a brother, and Selah, overlooking Laura's special needs and speech problems, is equally excited. But Sandra and I, as we read over Laura's varied diagnoses, aren't as sure. The girl's special needs place her in the most restrictive educational setting allowed in school, there are doubts about her cognitive abilities, possible autism, the various medications she's taken. Her treatment has been inconsistent, probably due to her moving around so often. Doctors change, therapists change, schools and foster parents change—and with every change, the approach to treating her changes.

As a result of all this reading, a certain amount of fear settles on us. But fear is always a bad advisor—we continue the visits, praying that what Laura truly needs are two dedicated parents and a loving family, people in her life that will never give her up or give up on her. And so, our weekend visits continue, our goal to have Kenneth and Laura come to live with us by the end of the school year.

On the last day of school, its arranged that Laura and Kenneth will be brought over by their foster parents. We've planned a gala homecoming, posters and balloons welcoming them as they drive up, friends and family, caseworker, adoption specialist, all cheering their arrival. Then it's into the backyard, where we've set out piles of food, mounds of dessert, napkins and paper plates and the finest of plastic utensils. No fatted calf, but that's only because none of the local food stores sell them. We gather around Laura and

Kenneth, praying a blessing, and thanking the foster families who have cared so well for them over the past year. Then we feast!

Sitting at the makeshift tables, surrounded by friends, children, family, other foster parents... that's when I know Sandra and I have made the right decision, the decision God wanted us to make. Because people are happy, laughing, the kids grinning. Without a doubt, doing what God asks can be hard, weary work. But the fruits of the Spirit, the fruits I now see bubbling up all around me, these can only come from God. I sit back, thinking about nearly two decades of infertility, about the heartache and struggle, and I say a silent prayer. Thank you, Lord, for allowing us to sit at this table. A table You've set for us.

A slightly different reality hits me the next morning. It's the first day of summer, I wake to ten kids with no schoolwork. We have a plan, of course—I'm scheduled to be a guest speaker at several kids' camps, we need to set off almost immediately. The problem is, our RV comfortably sleeps eight, uncomfortably sleeps ten, and no way at all sleeps twelve. So, in our travels to and from the different camps, we're forced to improvise. Tents are fun... unless it rains, something it does rather often throughout the Florida summer. Sometimes we sport a hotel room or borrow a cabin. Once, we all camped out in a church, bundling up on the floor.

The positive spin is, not knowing exactly where we'll be sleeping is an experience that helps us all bond. That's the way I view it. Sandra's view is somewhat different. Taking ten kids to the supermarket is a trial—taking them on road trips demands a level of organization I can't quite grasp. There's food and nap schedules and all the routines that at home are simple enough. But in an RV? Driving to a different camp each week? Jesus says that the kingdom of Heaven belongs to these little ones, but I'm betting He's got a cushy place set aside for all the moms who help them along.

Another bonding experience is the challenge of coming up with new names for Kenneth and Laura. Once we've explained that the names need to begin with the letter 'S', Kenneth quickly makes his choice be known. He wants to be called 'Superman'.

"Slight problem there, son," I say, wrapping an arm around his shoulder. "Copyright infringement."

The problem is, there are only so many names in the bible starting with 'S'. Laura comes up with the name, Sophia. Though it's not used in the Bible as a name, the word appears often, for Sophia, in Greek, means wisdom. As Jesus grew in wisdom, we are hoping that our new Sophia will also.

It's Samuel who finds the right name for his new brother. "How about Solomon? He was wise. And rich!"

Kenneth likes the name, and that's the end of it. Or rather, the beginning of it. Sophia and Solomon, two versions of wisdom.

And then it's off to the next kids camp, the next adventure in finding a place to sleep. In this, I'm probably the biggest kid around. I love being away from the distractions of television and technology, surrounded instead by the magnificence of God's creation. No wonder so many kids discover Jesus in these camps. He's always very near, but in the quiet and beauty of nature, it's impossible not to feel His closeness. In this setting, some kids are healed of physical ailments, some invite Him to be the Lord and Savior of their lives. A few even dedicate their lives to full-time ministry, aspiring to church ministry positions and missions work.

For me, it's a summer of miracles. Ten of them, each and everyone a miracle. I often think back twenty years, to my first date with Sandra. What if I had told her, when she'd asked of my plans and dreams, that I wanted to adopt ten kids? Would she still have considered marriage? Or, positions reversed, would I? Probably not, for I would not have believed I could do it. And I haven't.

God has done this, and it is marvelous in our eyes.

Solomon and Sophia's Adoption Day.

Chapter Fourteen

The Church is the Answer

In his first letter to the Corinthians, Paul tells them, *You were bought at a price.* As adoptive parents, Sandra and I have many times stood before a judge, and one of the questions asked is, "Can you provide for this child?" For a private adoption, legal and other fees can be quite exorbitant. But even when adopting through the foster care system, there are sometimes lawyers' fees, court fees, various other expenses, as well as the expenditure of time, effort, and the disruption of what once had been a comfortable and predictable life.

Whatever the costs, they are borne without any guarantee of success. We strive to offer our adopted children a good life, but sometimes, all we accomplish through our endless hours of struggle is to lift a child away from suicide. Or from addiction. Or from prostitution. Though we would wish it otherwise, sometimes our role is limited to this—we give them the gift of choice.

Before a child can be considered for adoption, the birth parents' rights to that child must be severed completely. Once a judge does this, there is no going back. In the eyes of the law, that child is now an orphan, with no inheritance, no legacy, no way to ever reclaim his birthright. If no one adopts him, he will live in a foster home or group home until he turns eighteen. The statistics on kids who 'age out' of foster care are horrific. 50% will not graduate high school, over 60% will be unemployed for more than a year before they turn twenty. A third will be homeless in two to three years, and another 30% will do jail time.

For the ones who are adopted, it's a different story. In court, in front of many witnesses, the judge bangs down his gavel and tells the parents, "This is now your child, as if naturally born to you." The child is given a new name and a new inheritance. The birth certificate arriving a few weeks later will testify to this—his old name will not appear on the document, nor will the names of his birth parents. In a very real way, the old has vanished, a new name has been given to him, new parents, a new life, new possibilities.

Why am I telling you all this? Because the adoption process I've described is almost identical to the spiritual adoption we undergo through salvation. We have all sinned and fallen short of the glory of God. Through Adam, our parental rights were severed. For a very long time, humankind wandered hopelessly through life, without joy or peace or contentment, orphans in the truest sense of the word. Then Jesus saw us. "Father," he said. "Let me care for these lost sheep. Let me provide for them, show them the way. Let me bring healing to the broken, hope to those in despair, light to those walking in darkness."

His Father, the Almighty Judge, answered him. "A

price must be paid, Son."

"Let me pay it, Father. Please. My life for theirs."

With only a hint of sadness, the Judge brought down his mighty gavel. "It is done!" And the world was forever changed. Because now, when God looks at our spiritual birth certificates, He sees a new name and a new creation, one washed clean of sin and made white as snow. All our faults and failures have been forgiven, for the name of Jesus is boldly written across the bottom line. The Son has claimed us, the price has been paid by His very blood.

But here's the catch—there's still no guarantee of success. The gift has been given, and it will never be taken from us. But we have a choice. Accept the gift and follow Him who gave it. Or turn away. Just as no one can force an adopted child to accept the love and guidance you offer them, no one can force you to accept the love and guidance offered by Jesus.

Now here are two interesting facts. This might seem a departure from what's being discussed, but I assure you it is not. The first fact—70% of all Americans identify themselves as Christians. They say they believe in God, believe in His Son. Here's the second fact—about 20,000 teenage orphans age out of foster care each year.

How can both be true? The Bible commands us over and over again to care for orphans. With the overwhelming number of people in America claiming to be followers of Christ, this should be no problem. Yet how many churches have an active Orphan Care ministry? How many have weekly groups devoted to helping foster and adoptive families, relative and non-relative caregivers? How many hours of their week do pastors, ministers, priests dedicate to this type of family ministry? When I ask these questions, what I too often receive back are platitudes and excuses.

"Oh, the government takes care of those things."

"I can't even handle my own kids."

"Our church has an annual food and clothing drive."

"We've formed an organization that does wonderful work collecting and distributing funds."

"We support global orphan care ministry."

A scene comes to mind—Jesus has just delivered his sermon on the mount, he's walking down the hill, followed by a large crowd. Suddenly the crowd parts, for a man with leprosy is coming. The leper, covered with scaly and bloody rags, kneels at the feet of Jesus. "Lord," he says, his voice broken as the rest of him, "if you are willing, you can make me clean."

Jesus quickly takes a double-step backward, afraid that he, too, might contract the dreaded disease. He grabs Judas, his treasurer, and points to the man kneeling before him. "We donate to a leprosy research organization, right? Let's do our best to make this man clean—double our contribution!"

Thank God, this isn't what happened. When asked if he was willing, Jesus reached out and touched the leper. Since leprosy is spread by touch, this simple action was sure to send an electric ripple through the crowd. No one touched a leper. Heal him if you're willing, sure—but don't *touch* him.

Orphans, too, need to be touched. They need to be held and cuddled and sung to sleep. They need to be given a childhood.

I heard the voice of the Lord saying, "Whom shall I send? Who will go for us?"

And I said, "Here am I. Send me!"

Approximately 20,000 teens a year age out of a foster home, entering the world with no hope, no future, no family to return to should they stumble. They disappear from our sight, from our thoughts, and from our prayers.

Here's another thought to consider—many of you believe abortion to be wrong. You believe it to be an abomination and a travesty, and that someday, we as a nation will be judged for it. Many of you pray daily for an end to abortion. Perhaps you write letters, or donate to Pro-Life candidates, or attend anti-abortion rallies. I certainly do. But what if our prayers are answered? What if abortion is declared illegal? Who will care for the 3,000 unwanted babies daily saved from a premature death? As a church, are we ready? And if not, why bother to pray? Beseeching God is great, it's wonderful—but we must also back up our prayers with a willingness to do His work.

With all my heart, I believe that as a Church, we can save those teens who have never found a home. We can save those babies who, without us, will never be given a choice, because they'll never be given a life. But the task will not be easy. And it certainly will not be comfortable.

Jesus tells us that we will not be left as orphans, for he will send the Holy Spirit to comfort us. In times of trouble, I have felt the Comforter's presence wrap around me, a warm blanket when the world is cold, a hand on my shoulder when I'm scared, the touch of heaven when everything around me appears to be going to hell. Truly, I am never alone.

But I am often confused. Why is it that the Holy Spirit, the great Comforter, seems so intent on sending me in a direction away from my comfort zone? Sandra and I could have stopped adopting children after Silas. Nothing wrong with a single child, one precious being to lavish all our love upon. With a single child, we would fit, we would be one more practical couple not wishing to jeopardize our upwardly mobile life-track. Isn't that what the American Dream is all about, hard-working people seeking a comfortable middle-class life?

Instead, the Comforter sent us into deep waters, with the promise that we would always stay afloat. Jesus might seem asleep, but our small boat would survive whatever storms came our way. Just have faith. And so Sandra and I prayed a dangerous prayer. "Lord, give us as many kids as You want us to have. Our lives are not our own."

In our safe, risk-free culture, most people, Christians included, desire a life of ease and security. Opening your home to a foster child with a willingness to adopt if that's what God calls you to do—well, that's never going to be a safe and easy path. No, it's a dangerous decision. In fact, it's the most dangerous decision you can make, to give your will over to God. It may well turn your world upside down. Who knows, it may turn everyone's world upside down. It's happened before.

Think of Mary's dangerous decision to accept God's will and give birth to God's son. Think of Joseph's decision to accept Mary as his wife, to support this miraculous birth.

Think of John and James leaving their lives and their livelihoods to follow Jesus. Or Peter, despite the shame of three times denying Christ, standing up on the day of Pentecost to preach Christ's message. Or millions of other Christians who over the years have stepped out in faith, crying to our Lord, *Send me!* The Holy Spirit has never once deserted even a single one of these disciples.

Which hardly means that the great Comforter has granted them a life of comfort. Not in a worldly way, at least. Love, joy, peace, patience... the fruits of the Spirit are of no worth at your local bank, they'll do nothing to increase your 401K. Mary did not give herself a life of ease when she willingly agreed to carry and care for God's only Son. Quite the opposite. In just the same way, opening your home to a foster child will undoubtedly complicate your life. It's a bold and courageous decision, this stepping out to do God's will.

Before saying yes, Satan will undoubtedly put into your mind all the good and practical reasons for withholding your offering to God—you're too old, you're just starting your own family, the house is too small, there's too little money, you have too many other commitments... once you start down the road of excuses, the list is endless.

The other road is simpler. Narrower. And far more dangerous. Once the first step is taken, you may never be comfortable again. But you will always be comforted.

Say that prayer today. *Send me.* Then open your heart and your home to a foster child, and see where God takes you. And if you're not called to take in a foster child, pray about launching an orphan care ministry in your church, mentoring a biological parent who is trying to get their child back from foster care, becoming a Guardian ad Litem (CASA in some states), so you can be a voice for a child in the courtroom, bringing a meal to a foster family, providing babysitting or respite...

Not everyone is called to foster or adopt, but everyone can do something!

(For a research-based comprehensive foster care ministry model, go to compact.family, *to find a CompaCare representative in your area.)*